Ninja CREAMi H Protein Power Cookbook

Boost Up Your Body with Delicious & Healthy Frozen Recipes for Fitness & Flavor (Deluxe Desserts)

Patrick Allen

Copyright © 2024 by Patrick Allen

All rights reserved. Unauthorized reproduction of any part of this book is strictly prohibited without prior written consent from the publisher or author, except as permitted by applicable copyright law.

This publication aims to provide accurate and authoritative information on the subject matter covered. It is sold with the understanding that neither the author nor the publisher is offering legal, investment, accounting, or other professional services. While every effort has been made by the author and publisher to ensure the accuracy and completeness of the contents of this book, they do not warrant or guarantee its accuracy or completeness and disclaim any implied warranties of merchantability or fitness for a particular purpose. No warranty, express or implied, is made by the publisher or author regarding the information contained herein.

MY SINCERE GRATITUDE TO YOU

Thank you for choosing this book and making it part of your culinary journey. Your trust in my High-Protein recipes for the Ninja Creami means so much to me, and I am deeply grateful for your support.

This book is the result of countless hours of experimenting, and knowing these recipes will bring joy to your kitchen fills me with pride and gratitude. I hope they inspire creativity and excitement in your culinary adventures.

Your support fuels my passion and motivates me to keep exploring and sharing new ideas. Thank you for allowing my recipes to play a part in your journey.

As you explore these pages, I hope you find inspiration and create delicious memories. Happy creating and enjoying every moment!

With Love

Patrick Allen

This Cookbook Belongs to

_____

_____

_____

About the Author

Patrick Allen is a New York-based chef, author, and restaurateur who champions the idea that the right kitchen tools can transform cooking into a joyful and effortless experience.

With a passion for culinary innovation, Patrick has penned several renowned books on mastering kitchen devices to create mouthwatering recipes, making him a trusted voice for home cooks and professionals alike.

When not writing or exploring new recipes, Patrick can be found at his small upscale restaurant, where he combines his love for fresh ingredients and modern techniques to delight diners. His work reflects a deep commitment to simplifying and elevating everyday cooking.

He resides in New York City with his wife, two children, and their beloved dog.

Always Remember that:

A device is only as good as how you use it. may your kitchen be filled with creativity, joy, and delicious moments

CONTENTS

INTRODUCTION 1
- Why Ninja CREAMi? Unlocking the Power of Frozen Nutrition 3
- Understanding Protein: How It Fuels Your Body 5
- Essential Ingredients List & Substitutions for High-Protein Treats................ 7
- Mastering the Ninja CREAMi – Tips & Tricks for Perfect Consistency! 10

CHAPTER 1: ICE CREAM DELIGHTS... 13
- Vanilla Bean Protein Power Ice Cream 13
- Double Chocolate Fudge Protein Ice Cream 13
- Peanut Butter Cup Protein Ice Cream 14
- Cookies & Cream Muscle Ice Cream 14
- Mocha Espresso High-Protein Ice Cream 15
- Cinnamon Roll Swirl Protein Ice Cream 15
- Chocolate Banana Recovery Ice Cream 16
- Salted Caramel Whey Ice Cream 16
- Birthday Cake Protein Ice Cream 17
- Maple Pecan Crunch Protein Ice Cream 17
- Peanut Butter Drizzle (Low-Fat) Ice Cream 18
- Matcha Green Tea Protein Ice Cream 18
- Espresso-Cocoa Dusting Ice Cream 19

CHAPTER 2: ICE CREAM MIX-INS... 20
- Crushed Protein Bar Chunks Ice Cream 20
- Sugar-Free Chocolate Chips & Cocoa Nibs Ice Cream................................. 21
- Strawberry Cheesecake Protein Ice Cream 22
- Toasted Coconut & Almonds Ice Cream 23
- Chia & Flax Seed Crunch Ice Cream 24
- High-Protein Brownie Bites Ice Cream 25
- Oatmeal Cookie Protein Crumbles Ice Cream 26
- Collagen-Boosted Granola Clusters Ice Cream 27
- Cinnamon Toasted Pecans Ice Cream 28
- Sugar-Free Marshmallow Swirls Ice Cream 29
- Crushed Freeze-Dried Berries Ice Cream 30

CHAPTER 3: SMOOTHIE BOWL DELIGHTS 31
  Tropical Mango Pineapple Protein Bowl 31
  Acai Superfood Protein Bowl 31
  Chocolate Almond Butter Energy Bowl 32
  Berry Blast Greek Yogurt Protein Bowl 32
  Peanut Butter Banana Muscle Bowl 33
  Green Machine Spinach Protein Bowl 33
  Vanilla Coconut Crunch Smoothie Bowl 34
  Mocha Oatmeal Protein Bowl 34
  Strawberry Kiwi Power Bowl 35
  Blueberry Vanilla Whey Bowl 35
  Apple Pie Cinnamon Protein Bowl 36

CHAPTER 4: GELATO 37
  Italian Vanilla Bean Whey Gelato 37
  Dark Chocolate Hazelnut Protein Gelato 37
  Pistachio Almond Cream Gelato 38
  Espresso Macchiato Protein Gelato 38
  Coconut Cashew High-Protein Gelato 39
  Tiramisu Collagen-Boosted Gelato 39
  Raspberry Chocolate Swirl Protein Gelato 40
  Honey Lavender Protein Gelato 40
  Lemon Ricotta Whey Gelato 41
  Maple Walnut High-Protein Gelato 41
  Chai Spice Protein Gelato 42
  Black Sesame Whey Gelato 42

CHAPTER 5: SORBETS 43
  Pineapple Ginger Recovery Sorbet 43
  Raspberry Lemonade Whey Sorbet 43
  Watermelon Mint Electrolyte Sorbet 44
  Peach Mango Collagen Sorbet 44
  Strawberry Basil High-Protein Sorbet 45
  Blueberry Acai Superfood Sorbet 45
  Lemon Coconut Protein Sorbet 46

Passionfruit Orange Muscle Sorbet 46
Blackberry Lime Whey Sorbet 47
Tart Cherry Vanilla Recovery Sorbet 47
Honeydew Green Tea Sorbet 48
Cucumber Melon Refresh Sorbet 48

CHAPTER 6: MILKSHAKES 49
Classic Vanilla Whey Power Shake 49
Double Chocolate Casein Shake 50
Peanut Butter Banana Recovery Shake 51
Cookies & Cream Whey Shake 52
Strawberry Shortcake Protein Shake 53
Mocha Cold Brew Muscle Shake 54
Cinnamon Roll Oatmeal Shake 55
Dark Chocolate Cherry Power Shake 56
Chai Latte Collagen Shake 57
Caramel Macchiato Whey Shake 58
Key Lime Pie Protein Shake 59
Pumpkin Spice Recovery Shake 60

MEASUREMENT CONVERSION TABLE 61
CONCLUSION 62
RECIPES INDEX 64

INTRODUCTION

If you've ever thought that healthy eating means giving up your favorite desserts, think again! Welcome to the High-Protein Revolution, where indulgence meets nutrition, and every frozen treat you make fuels your body with the protein it craves. Get ready to indulge in a whole new way!

A few years ago, protein-rich desserts were almost unheard of outside of chalky shakes or dry protein bars. But everything changed when fitness enthusiasts, athletes, and home cooks started experimenting with the power of frozen protein treats. What was once a niche idea quickly became a movement—one where people realized they didn't have to choose between fueling their bodies and enjoying their favorite sweets.

Take, for example, a small café in New York that struggled to keep up with demand for its homemade frozen yogurt. Customers wanted healthier options but weren't satisfied with the taste of low-calorie, low-protein alternatives. When they introduced a high-protein frozen yogurt, made with Greek yogurt, whey protein, and natural ingredients, it became their best-selling item. Why? because it delivered both nutrition and flavor—a game changer for dessert lovers and fitness-minded customers alike.

Why High-Protein Desserts?

- **Muscle Recovery & Strength** – Protein supports muscle growth, repair, and recovery after workouts.

- **Sustained Energy** – Unlike sugar-loaded treats, protein helps keep you full longer and stabilizes blood sugar.

- **Metabolism Boosting** – A higher protein intake can aid in fat loss by increasing thermogenesis and reducing cravings.

- **Gut & Immune Health** – Many protein sources, like Greek yogurt and cottage cheese, contain probiotics and essential amino acids.

With the Ninja CREAMi, you get total control over your ingredients, allowing you to craft high-protein treats tailored to your macros, dietary needs, and flavor preferences. Say goodbye to boring protein shakes and hello to creamy, delicious, and satisfying frozen delights! You're in the driver's seat of your dessert journey.

This book will show you how to use simple ingredients, science-backed nutrition, and your Ninja CREAMi to transform the way you enjoy high-protein treats. Are you ready to revolutionize the way you fuel your body? Let's dive into the recipes and unlock the full potential of your Ninja CREAMi High-Protein Power Cookbook! Get ready to unleash your inner dessert artist.

Why Ninja CREAMi? Unlocking the Power of Frozen Nutrition

Frozen desserts have always been a treat we enjoy—something we grab when we want to indulge—but they can sometimes interfere with our health goals. The Ninja CREAMi makes a difference. This isn't just an ice cream maker; it's a revolutionary tool for anyone wanting to enjoy high-protein, healthy, and tasty frozen desserts.

Picture this: you can choose every ingredient in your ice cream, smoothie bowl, or sorbet. You get to decide how much sugar to add, increase the protein, and leave out any preservatives or fillers that are often in store-bought versions. If you're an athlete, a fitness lover, or just someone who enjoys ice cream but seeks a healthier option, the Ninja CREAMi allows you to make frozen treats that meet your nutritional needs while still tasting great and having a nice texture.

The Science Behind CREAMi Magic

Traditional ice cream makers use churning, which requires extra fats and stabilizers to create a creamy texture. The Ninja CREAMi features special spinning blade technology that finely shaves frozen ingredients, creating a smooth and creamy texture. Thus, you can get the texture of real ice cream without using heavy cream or too much sugar.

What Makes the Ninja CREAMi Perfect for High-Protein Treats?

1. **Total Control Over Macros** – Adjust protein, fat, and carb content based on your goals.
2. **Creamy, Dairy-Free & Low-Carb Options** – Works just as well with **Greek yogurt, almond milk, whey, casein, and plant-based proteins**.
3. **No Preservatives or Fillers** – Unlike store-bought protein ice creams, you won't find any gums, artificial stabilizers, or mystery ingredients.
4. **Versatility Beyond Ice Cream** – Make **smoothie bowls, protein-packed sorbets, and even recovery blends** that work for your post-workout nutrition.
5. **Easy, Single-Serve Convenience** – Prep your protein mix, freeze overnight, and spin fresh whenever you're ready!

From Ordinary to High-Protein Superfood

Think about this: a regular scoop of ice cream contains around 20-25g of sugar and very little protein. Using the Ninja CREAMi, you can quickly make chocolate peanut butter protein ice cream that has more than 25g of protein in each serving and much less sugar.

This book will show you how to make the most of your Ninja CREAMi, transforming basic ingredients into healthy, protein-rich frozen treats. If you're looking for a tasty protein bowl after your workout, a low-carb keto dessert, or a dairy-free frozen treat, the Ninja CREAMi is the perfect solution.

Let's explore the ingredients, methods, and recipes to help you create tasty and healthy CREAMi dishes!

Understanding Protein: How It Fuels Your Body

Protein is frequently referred to as the building block of life, and there's a solid reason for that. It is essential for muscle growth, repairing tissues, producing hormones, and maintaining energy levels. If you're an athlete wanting to recover after exercising, aiming to keep a lean body, or just looking to feel full and energized all day, protein is key for keeping your body strong, healthy, and working well.

Why Is Protein So Important?

All the cells in your body depend on protein. Protein differs from fats and carbohydrates because it isn't stored in the body for later use. This means you need to include it in your diet regularly. When you eat protein, your body breaks it down into amino acids, which assist:

- **Repair & Build Muscle** – Essential for recovery after exercise and maintaining lean muscle mass.
- **Boost Metabolism** – Digesting protein requires more energy, helping you burn more calories naturally.
- **Keep You Full Longer** – Reduces cravings and helps with appetite control.
- **Support Healthy Skin, Hair & Nails** – Protein is the foundation for collagen, which keeps your body looking and feeling strong.
- **Enhance Immune Function** – Key amino acids strengthen your immune system and help your body fight illness.

How Much Protein Do You Really Need?

The recommended protein intake varies depending on **activity level, age, and fitness goals**. A general guideline:

- **Sedentary individuals**: ~0.36g per pound of body weight
- **Active individuals**: ~0.5–0.8g per pound
- **Athletes & muscle gain goals**: ~0.8–1.2g per pound

For example, if you weigh **150 lbs** and exercise regularly, aiming for **75-120g of protein daily** can help with muscle recovery and overall health.

Best Protein Sources for Frozen Treats

The Ninja CREAMi is great because it lets you mix high-protein ingredients into smooth, tasty frozen treats without needing extra sugar or unhealthy fats. Here are some great protein-rich ingredients for CREAMi recipes:

Greek Yogurt & Cottage Cheese: Naturally high in protein, with a creamy texture perfect for ice creams and smoothie bowls.

Whey & Casein Protein: Fast-digesting (whey) and slow-digesting (casein) proteins that add smoothness and richness.

Plant-Based Proteins: Pea, hemp, or soy protein for those following a vegan or dairy-free diet.

Egg Whites: A low-calorie, high-protein option that blends well for a fluffy texture.

Nut Butters & Seeds: Almond butter, peanut butter, chia seeds, and flaxseeds add protein and healthy fats.

Fueling Your Body the Delicious Way

When you add high-quality protein to your frozen desserts, you're creating a delicious treat that also supports your body's performance. Rather than depending on sugary ice creams that make you feel tired, your Ninja CREAMi lets you make protein-packed treats that energize you, help with your fitness, and keep you feeling full.

Next, let's look at the best ingredients and substitutes for making the perfect high-protein Ninja CREAMi recipes!

Essential Ingredients List & Substitutions for High-Protein Treats

Making high-protein frozen treats with the Ninja CREAMi is about finding the perfect mix of ingredients to get a creamy and tasty texture while boosting protein levels. This guide will help you find the best ingredients and their perfect substitutes, whether you want dairy-based, plant-based, keto-friendly, or low-sugar options.

Protein Bases: The Foundation of Your CREAMi Creations

These ingredients provide structure, creaminess, and protein in your frozen treats.

Best Protein Bases

Ingredient	Protein (per 1 cup)	Benefits
Greek Yogurt (Plain, 2% or Whole)	20g	Thick, tangy, and naturally creamy
Cottage Cheese	25g	Ultra-creamy, high in casein protein
Milk (Dairy or Plant-Based)	8g (dairy), 1-4g (plant-based)	Adds lightness and smooth blending
Silken Tofu	10g	Great plant-based, dairy-free alternative
Coconut Cream (Full-Fat)	5g	Rich and creamy, good for vegan options

Substitutions:

- Swap **Greek yogurt** for **cottage cheese** for a smoother, less tangy texture.
- Use **silken tofu** instead of dairy for a **plant-based protein boost**.
- Opt for **coconut cream** for a **dairy-free, keto-friendly option**.

Protein Powders: Boosting the Macros & Flavor

Adding protein powder helps achieve higher protein content while enhancing flavor.

Best Protein Powders for CREAMi Recipes

Type	Best For	Notes
Whey Protein Isolate	Creamy, smooth ice creams	Blends easily, fast digesting
Casein Protein	Thick, custard-like texture	Slow digesting, ultra-creamy
Pea or Soy Protein	Vegan, dairy-free options	Can be grainy—blend well
Collagen Peptides	Light, smooth consistency	No flavor, boosts skin & joint health
Egg White Protein	Low-fat, fluffy texture	Great for lower-calorie options

Tips for Success:

- **Mix protein powders with liquids** (milk, almond milk) before freezing to prevent clumping.
- **Casein works best for ice cream** due to its thickening properties.

- **Avoid plant-based proteins that are gritty**—blend well with nut butters or bananas for smoothness.

Natural Sweeteners: Enhancing Flavor Without the Sugar Crash

Most store-bought ice creams are packed with refined sugars, but you can achieve just as much sweetness with healthier alternatives.

Best Natural Sweeteners

Sweetener	Notes
Stevia	Zero-calorie, natural, very sweet (use sparingly)
Monk Fruit Sweetener	Keto-friendly, no aftertaste
Allulose	Behaves like sugar, prevents ice crystals
Erythritol	Low-calorie, slightly cooling effect
Honey/Maple Syrup	Natural but adds some carbs

Best Substitutions:

- Use allulose or monk fruit for a keto-friendly, low-glycemic option.
- Blend banana, dates, or honey for natural sweetness with added fiber

Healthy Fats: For Creaminess & Satiety

Fats improve texture and help keep you full longer.

Best Healthy Fats for CREAMi Recipes

Ingredient	Benefits
Nut Butters (Almond, Peanut, Cashew)	Rich texture, healthy fats, adds flavor
Coconut Cream or Full-Fat Coconut Milk	Dairy-free creaminess
Avocado	Mild taste, ultra-creamy consistency
Chia or Flax Seeds	Fiber-rich, slightly thickening

Best Substitutions:

- Swap heavy cream for coconut cream for a dairy-free alternative.
- Use avocado instead of nut butter for a milder, smoother fat source.

Texture Enhancers & Mix-Ins

These help improve consistency and add fun flavors and crunch.

Great Texture Enhancers

Ingredient	Purpose
Xanthan Gum (¼ teaspoon)	Prevents ice crystals, keeps texture smooth
Gelatin or Agar Agar	Adds thickness and stability
Banana or Pumpkin Puree	Natural thickness, subtle sweetness

Best Mix-Ins (Add After Spinning):

- Crushed nuts (almonds, pecans, peanuts)
- Dark chocolate chips (sugar-free for keto)
- Coconut flakes
- Granola or protein cereal pieces
- Crushed protein bars

Bringing It All Together

Using the right combination of protein, healthy fats, and natural sweeteners will help you create delicious, high-protein frozen treats that fit your dietary goals. Whether you're making a muscle-recovery ice cream, a keto-friendly dessert, or a dairy-free sorbet, these ingredient swaps will keep your Ninja CREAMi creations nutritious, satisfying, and packed with flavor.

Mastering the Ninja CREAMi – Tips & Tricks for Perfect Consistency!

Making a delicious high-protein frozen treat with the Ninja CREAMi involves more than simply putting ingredients into a pint and freezing them. The right techniques will give you smooth, creamy, and scoopable results—avoiding icy, chalky, or overly soft textures.

Check out these great tips and tricks to ensure every batch of high-protein ice cream, smoothie bowl, or sorbet tastes just as good as (or even better than!) what you find in stores.

1. The Freezing Process: Set Yourself Up for Success

Always Freeze for 24 Hours

- Your base needs to be fully solid before spinning for the best results.
- Freezing at 0°F (-18°C) or lower prevents ice crystals from forming.
- Avoid placing the pint near the freezer door where temperature fluctuates.

Fill the Pint to the Max Fill Line

- Too much air space can cause uneven freezing and affect texture.
- For smaller servings, use multiple pints instead of underfilling one.

Use Cold Ingredients List Before Freezing

- If you heat or blend ingredients, chill the mixture first before freezing.
- Warm mixtures take longer to freeze and may not process correctly.

2. The Spin Cycle: How to Get the Creamiest Texture

Always Start with the ICE CREAM or LITE ICE CREAM Function

- **Ice Cream**: Best for full-fat, creamy bases with dairy.
- **Lite Ice Cream**: Ideal for low-fat, high-protein, or alternative bases.

If It's Too Icy or Hard, Use the RE-SPIN Function

- Protein-heavy bases (like whey or casein) can freeze harder than traditional ice cream.
- Use the Re-Spin button once or twice if the first spin isn't creamy enough.

If Still Too Hard After Re-Spin, Add a Splash of Liquid

- Add 1-2 tablespoon of milk, almond milk, or coconut milk to loosen the texture.
- Re-spin again to bring everything together smoothly.

Don't Over-Re-Spin!

- Two re-spins max—any more can make the mixture too soft and melt too quickly.
- If still too hard after two re-spins, let it sit at room temperature for 5-10 minutes, then re-spin.

3. Ingredient Ratios: Preventing Ice Crystals & Chalky Texture

Use Enough Fat for a Creamier Texture

- Low-fat bases freeze harder—use at least 1 tablespoon of a healthy fat (nut butter, coconut cream, or avocado).
- Greek yogurt and cottage cheese need balancing fats for smoothness.

Balance Protein Powder Properly

- Too much whey protein can make the texture chalky or icy—stick to ½–1 scoop per pint.
- Casein protein blends better for a creamy consistency.
- Mix protein powder with liquid first before freezing to avoid clumps.

Use a Natural Thickener (Optional)

- A pinch of xanthan gum, guar gum, or gelatin (¼ teaspoon) helps prevent ice crystals.
- Bananas, pumpkin puree, or avocados naturally thicken while keeping the texture smooth.

4. Getting the Right Texture for Your Type of Treat

For Creamy, Scoopable Ice Cream

- Use a mix of Greek yogurt, cottage cheese, or full-fat coconut milk.
- Add 1 tablespoon of a healthy fat (nut butter, avocado, or heavy cream).
- Re-spin once or twice for extra smoothness.

For Smooth Sorbets

- Use 100% fruit purée or juice—avoid adding too much protein powder.
- A little allulose or monk fruit sweetener helps prevent iciness.
- If it is too icy, add a splash of water or juice and re-spin.

For Thick Smoothie Bowls

- Start with a high-protein base like Greek yogurt or a dairy-free alternative.
- Add a scoop of protein powder and blend well before freezing.
- If it is too firm after freezing, re-spin it with a splash of almond milk.

5. Storage & Serving: Keeping It Fresh & Scoopable

Store Pints with a Lid On to Prevent Freezer Burn

- Use the Ninja CREAMi pint lids or plastic wrap for a tight seal.
- Avoid storing in the door section of the freezer—keep it in the back where the temperature is more stable.

Let It Sit for a Few Minutes Before Scooping

- If too firm, leave the pint at room temperature for **5-10 minutes** before spinning or scooping.
- This helps soften the ice cream naturally without melting it too much.

Eat Within 3-5 Days for Best Texture

- Since homemade ice cream doesn't have preservatives, it's best enjoyed fresh.
- If stored longer, **let it thaw slightly and re-spin before serving**.

Final Thoughts: Mastering Your CREAMi Creations

Getting the hang of the Ninja CREAMi requires some practice, but once you learn the right techniques, you can make delicious, high-protein frozen treats with the ideal texture every time.

Now that you've learned the secrets to achieving perfect consistency, let's explore some of the best high-protein recipes to help you reach your fitness goals while satisfying your sweet cravings!

CHAPTER 1: ICE CREAM DELIGHTS

Vanilla Bean Protein Power Ice Cream

Time Needed to Prepare: 5 minutes
CREAMi Time: 2-3 minutes (plus re-spin if needed)
Number of Servings: 2

Ingredients List

- 1 cup of (240g) low-fat cottage cheese
- 1/2 cup of (120ml) unsweetened almond milk or skim milk
- 1 scoop (30g) vanilla whey protein isolate
- 1 tablespoon of allulose or monk fruit sweetener
- 1 teaspoon vanilla bean paste or pure vanilla extract
- 1/4 teaspoon xanthan gum

Instructions

1. In a blender, combine cottage cheese, almond milk, protein powder, sweetener, vanilla bean paste, and xanthan gum. Blend until completely smooth.
2. Pour the mixture into a Ninja CREAMi pint and secure the lid.
3. Freeze for 24 hours until solid.
4. Once frozen, place the pint into the Ninja CREAMi and lock it into the machine.
5. Select the "Lite Ice Cream" mode and process.
6. If the texture is too firm or crumbly, add 1-2 tablespoons of almond milk and press Re-Spin for extra creaminess.
7. Serve immediately or store in the freezer with a lid for later.

Nutritional Information (Per Serving)
Calories: 175
Fats: 3g | **Protein:** 26g

Double Chocolate Fudge Protein Ice Cream

Time Needed to Prepare: 5 minutes
CREAMi Time: 2-3 minutes (plus re-spin if needed)
Number of Servings: 2

Ingredients List

- 1 cup of (240g) low-fat cottage cheese
- 1/2 cup of (120ml) unsweetened almond milk or skim milk
- 1 scoop (30g) chocolate whey protein isolate
- 1 tablespoon of unsweetened cocoa powder
- 1 tablespoon of allulose or monk fruit sweetener
- 1 teaspoon vanilla extract
- 1/4 teaspoon xanthan gum

Instructions

1. In a blender, combine cottage cheese, almond milk, protein powder, cocoa powder, sweetener, vanilla extract, and xanthan gum. Blend until completely smooth.
2. Pour the mixture into a Ninja CREAMi pint and secure the lid.
3. Freeze for 24 hours until solid.
4. Once frozen, place the pint into the Ninja CREAMi and lock it into the machine.
5. Select the "Lite Ice Cream" mode and process.
6. If the texture is too firm or crumbly, add 1-2 tablespoons of almond milk and press Re-Spin for extra creaminess.
7. Serve immediately or store in the freezer with a lid for later.

Nutritional Information (Per Serving)
Calories: 185
Fats: 4g
Protein: 27g

Peanut Butter Cup Protein Ice Cream

Time Needed to Prepare: 5 minutes
CREAMi Time: 2-3 minutes (plus re-spin if needed)
Number of Servings: 2

Ingredients List

- 1 cup of (240g) low-fat cottage cheese
- 1/2 cup of (120ml) unsweetened almond milk or skim milk
- 1 scoop (30g) chocolate whey protein isolate
- 1 tablespoon of unsweetened cocoa powder
- 1 tablespoon of natural peanut butter (no added sugar or oil)
- 1 tablespoon of allulose or monk fruit sweetener
- 1 teaspoon vanilla extract
- 1/4 teaspoon xanthan gum

Instructions

1. In a blender, combine cottage cheese, almond milk, protein powder, cocoa powder, peanut butter, sweetener, vanilla extract, and xanthan gum. Blend until completely smooth.
2. Pour the mixture into a Ninja CREAMi pint and secure the lid.
3. Freeze for 24 hours until solid.
4. Once frozen, place the pint into the Ninja CREAMi and lock it into the machine.
5. Select the "Lite Ice Cream" mode and process.
6. If the texture is too firm or crumbly, add 1-2 tablespoons of almond milk and press Re-Spin for extra creaminess.
7. Serve immediately or store in the freezer with a lid for later.

Nutritional Information (Per Serving)
Fats: 7g
Protein: 28g

Cookies & Cream Muscle Ice Cream

Time Needed to Prepare: 5 minutes
CREAMi Time: 2-3 minutes (plus re-spin if needed)
Number of Servings: 2

Ingredients List

- 1 cup of (240g) low-fat cottage cheese
- 1/2 cup of (120ml) unsweetened almond milk or skim milk
- 1 scoop (30g) cookies & cream whey protein isolate
- 1 tablespoon of allulose or monk fruit sweetener
- 1/2 teaspoon vanilla extract
- 1/4 teaspoon xanthan gum
- 2 chocolate sandwich cookies (crushed)

Instructions

1. In a blender, combine cottage cheese, almond milk, protein powder, sweetener, vanilla extract, and xanthan gum. Blend until completely smooth.
2. Pour the mixture into a Ninja CREAMi pint and secure the lid.
3. Freeze for 24 hours until solid.
4. Once frozen, place the pint into the Ninja CREAMi and lock it into the machine.
5. Select the "Lite Ice Cream" mode and process.
6. If the texture is too firm or crumbly, add 1-2 tablespoons of almond milk and press Re-Spin for extra creaminess.
7. Once smooth, add the crushed cookies and press the Mix-In button.
8. Serve immediately or store in the freezer with a lid for later.

Nutritional Information (Per Serving)
Calories: 210
Fats: 6g | **Protein:** 27g

Mocha Espresso High-Protein Ice Cream

Time Needed to Prepare: 5 minutes
CREAMi Time: 2-3 minutes (plus re-spin if needed)
Number of Servings: 2

Ingredients List

- 1 cup of (240g) low-fat cottage cheese
- 1/2 cup of (120ml) unsweetened almond milk or skim milk
- 1 scoop (30g) chocolate whey protein isolate
- 1 tablespoon of unsweetened cocoa powder
- 1 tablespoon of allulose or monk fruit sweetener
- 1 teaspoon instant espresso powder
- 1/2 teaspoon vanilla extract
- 1/4 teaspoon xanthan gum

Instructions

1. In a blender, combine cottage cheese, almond milk, protein powder, cocoa powder, sweetener, espresso powder, vanilla extract, and xanthan gum. Blend until completely smooth.
2. Pour the mixture into a Ninja CREAMi pint and secure the lid.
3. Freeze for 24 hours until solid.
4. Once frozen, place the pint into the Ninja CREAMi and lock it into the machine.
5. Select the "Lite Ice Cream" mode and process.
6. If the texture is too firm or crumbly, add 1-2 tablespoons of almond milk and press Re-Spin for extra creaminess.
7. Serve immediately or store in the freezer with a lid for later.

Nutritional Information (Per Serving)
Calories: 190
Fats: 4g
Protein: 27g

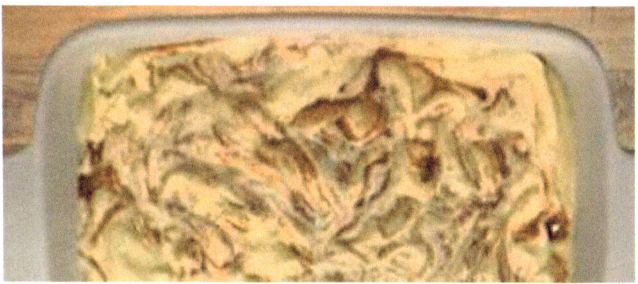

Cinnamon Roll Swirl Protein Ice Cream

Time Needed to Prepare: 5 minutes
CREAMi Time: 2-3 minutes (plus re-spin if needed)
Number of Servings: 2

Ingredients List

- 1 cup of (240g) low-fat cottage cheese
- 1/2 cup of (120ml) unsweetened almond milk or skim milk
- 1 scoop (30g) vanilla whey protein isolate
- 1 tablespoon of allulose or monk fruit sweetener
- 1 teaspoon vanilla extract
- 1/2 teaspoon ground cinnamon
- 1/4 teaspoon xanthan gum
- 1 teaspoon sugar-free maple syrup (for swirl)
- 1/2 teaspoon cinnamon mixed with 1/2 teaspoon allulose (for swirl)

Instructions

1. In a blender, combine cottage cheese, almond milk, protein powder, sweetener, vanilla extract, ground cinnamon, and xanthan gum. Blend until completely smooth.
2. Pour the mixture into a Ninja CREAMi pint and secure the lid.
3. Freeze for 24 hours until solid.
4. Once frozen, place the pint into the Ninja CREAMi and lock it into the machine.
5. Select the "Lite Ice Cream" mode and process.
6. If the texture is too firm or crumbly, add 1-2 tablespoons of almond milk and press Re-Spin for extra creaminess.
7. After re-spinning, drizzle sugar-free maple syrup and cinnamon-allulose mixture on top, then use the Mix-In function to create the swirl effect (optional, you can just drizzle it on top).
8. Serve immediately or store in the freezer with a lid for later.

Nutritional Information (Per Serving)
Calories: 185
Fats: 3.5g | **Protein:** 26g

Chocolate Banana Recovery Ice Cream

Time Needed to Prepare: 5 minutes
CREAMi Time: 2-3 minutes (plus re-spin if needed)
Number of Servings: 2

Ingredients List

- 1 cup of (240g) low-fat cottage cheese
- 1/2 cup of (120ml) unsweetened almond milk or skim milk
- 1 scoop (30g) chocolate whey protein isolate
- 1 tablespoon of unsweetened cocoa powder
- 1 small ripe banana (mashed)
- 1 tablespoon of allulose or monk fruit sweetener
- 1/2 teaspoon vanilla extract
- 1/4 teaspoon xanthan gum

Instructions

1. In a blender, combine cottage cheese, almond milk, protein powder, cocoa powder, mashed banana, sweetener, vanilla extract, and xanthan gum. Blend until completely smooth.
2. Pour the mixture into a Ninja CREAMi pint and secure the lid.
3. Freeze for 24 hours until solid.
4. Once frozen, place the pint into the Ninja CREAMi and lock it into the machine.
5. Select the "Lite Ice Cream" mode and process.
6. If the texture is too firm or crumbly, add 1-2 tablespoons of almond milk and press Re-Spin for extra creaminess.
7. Serve immediately or store in the freezer with a lid for later.

Nutritional Information (Per Serving)
Calories: 200
Fats: 4g
Protein: 26g

Salted Caramel Whey Ice Cream

Time Needed to Prepare: 5 minutes
CREAMi Time: 2-3 minutes (plus re-spin if needed)
Number of Servings: 2

Ingredients List

- 1 cup of (240g) low-fat cottage cheese
- 1/2 cup of (120ml) unsweetened almond milk or skim milk
- 1 scoop (30g) caramel whey protein isolate
- 1 tablespoon of sugar-free caramel syrup
- 1 tablespoon of allulose or monk fruit sweetener
- 1/2 teaspoon vanilla extract
- 1/8 teaspoon sea salt
- 1/4 teaspoon xanthan gum

Instructions

1. In a blender, combine cottage cheese, almond milk, protein powder, sugar-free caramel syrup, sweetener, vanilla extract, sea salt, and xanthan gum. Blend until completely smooth.
2. Pour the mixture into a Ninja CREAMi pint and secure the lid.
3. Freeze for 24 hours until solid.
4. Once frozen, place the pint into the Ninja CREAMi and lock it into the machine.
5. Select the "Lite Ice Cream" mode and process.
6. If the texture is too firm or crumbly, add 1-2 tablespoons of almond milk and press Re-Spin for extra creaminess.
7. Serve immediately or store in the freezer with a lid for later.

Nutritional Information (Per Serving)
Calories: 185
Fats: 3g | **Protein:** 27g

Birthday Cake Protein Ice Cream

Time Needed to Prepare: 5 minutes
CREAMi Time: 2-3 minutes (plus re-spin if needed)
Number of Servings: 2

Ingredients List

- 1 cup of (240g) low-fat cottage cheese
- 1/2 cup of (120ml) unsweetened almond milk or skim milk
- 1 scoop (30g) vanilla whey protein isolate
- 1 tablespoon of sugar-free vanilla pudding mix
- 1 tablespoon of allulose or monk fruit sweetener
- 1/2 teaspoon vanilla extract
- 1/4 teaspoon butter extract
- 1/4 teaspoon xanthan gum
- 1 teaspoon sugar-free rainbow sprinkles (for mix-in)

Instructions

1. In a blender, combine cottage cheese, almond milk, protein powder, pudding mix, sweetener, vanilla extract, butter extract, and xanthan gum. Blend until completely smooth.
2. Pour the mixture into a Ninja CREAMi pint and secure the lid.
3. Freeze for 24 hours until solid.
4. Once frozen, place the pint into the Ninja CREAMi and lock it into the machine.
5. Select the "Lite Ice Cream" mode and process.
6. If the texture is too firm or crumbly, add 1-2 tablespoons of almond milk and press Re-Spin for extra creaminess.
7. Once smooth, add sugar-free rainbow sprinkles and press the Mix-In button.
8. Serve immediately or store in the freezer with a lid for later.

Nutritional Information (Per Serving)
Calories: 190
Fats: 3.5g
Protein: 27g

Maple Pecan Crunch Protein Ice Cream

Time Needed to Prepare: 5 minutes
CREAMi Time: 2-3 minutes (plus re-spin if needed)
Number of Servings: 2

Ingredients List

- 1 cup of (240g) low-fat cottage cheese
- 1/2 cup of (120ml) unsweetened almond milk or skim milk
- 1 scoop (30g) vanilla whey protein isolate
- 1 tablespoon of sugar-free maple syrup
- 1 tablespoon of allulose or monk fruit sweetener
- 1/2 teaspoon vanilla extract
- 1/4 teaspoon butter extract
- 1/4 teaspoon xanthan gum
- 2 tablespoons of chopped toasted pecans (for mix-in)

Instructions

1. In a blender, combine cottage cheese, almond milk, protein powder, sugar-free maple syrup, sweetener, vanilla extract, butter extract, and xanthan gum. Blend until completely smooth.
2. Pour the mixture into a Ninja CREAMi pint and secure the lid.
3. Freeze for 24 hours until solid.
4. Once frozen, place the pint into the Ninja CREAMi and lock it into the machine.
5. Select the "Lite Ice Cream" mode and process.
6. If the texture is too firm or crumbly, add 1-2 tablespoons of almond milk and press Re-Spin for extra creaminess.
7. Once smooth, add chopped toasted pecans and press the Mix-In button.
8. Serve immediately or store in the freezer with a lid for later.

Nutritional Information (Per Serving)
Calories: 210
Fats: 6g
Protein: 26g

Peanut Butter Drizzle (Low-Fat) Ice Cream

Time Needed to Prepare: 5 minutes
CREAMi Time: 3-4 minutes (including Mix-In function)
Number of Servings: 2

Ingredients List

- 1 cup of (240g) low-fat cottage cheese
- 1/2 cup of (120ml) unsweetened almond milk or skim milk
- 1 scoop (30g) vanilla whey protein isolate
- 1 tablespoon of allulose or monk fruit sweetener
- 1/2 teaspoon vanilla extract
- 1/4 teaspoon xanthan gum
- 2 tablespoons of powdered peanut butter (mixed with 1-2 tablespoons of water for drizzle)

Instructions

1. In a blender, combine cottage cheese, almond milk, protein powder, sweetener, vanilla extract, and xanthan gum. Blend until completely smooth.
2. Pour the mixture into a Ninja CREAMi pint and secure the lid.
3. Freeze for 24 hours until solid.
4. Once frozen, place the pint into the Ninja CREAMi and lock it into the machine.
5. Select the "Lite Ice Cream" mode and process.
6. If the texture is too firm or crumbly, add 1-2 tablespoons of almond milk and press Re-Spin for extra creaminess.
7. In a small bowl, mix powdered peanut butter with water until smooth and drizzle over the ice cream.
8. Serve immediately or store in the freezer with a lid for later.

Nutritional Information (Per Serving)
Calories: 190
Fats: 4g
Protein: 28g

Matcha Green Tea Protein Ice Cream

Time Needed to Prepare: 5 minutes
CREAMi Time: 2-3 minutes (plus re-spin if needed)
Number of Servings: 2

Ingredients List

- 1 cup of (240g) low-fat cottage cheese
- 1/2 cup of (120ml) unsweetened almond milk or skim milk
- 1 scoop (30g) vanilla whey protein isolate
- 1 teaspoon high-quality matcha powder
- 1 tablespoon of allulose or monk fruit sweetener
- 1/2 teaspoon vanilla extract
- 1/4 teaspoon xanthan gum

Instructions

1. In a blender, combine cottage cheese, almond milk, protein powder, matcha powder, sweetener, vanilla extract, and xanthan gum. Blend until completely smooth.
2. Pour the mixture into a Ninja CREAMi pint and secure the lid.
3. Freeze for 24 hours until solid.
4. Once frozen, place the pint into the Ninja CREAMi and lock it into the machine.
5. Select the "Lite Ice Cream" mode and process.
6. If the texture is too firm or crumbly, add 1-2 tablespoons of almond milk and press Re-Spin for extra creaminess.
7. Serve immediately or store in the freezer with a lid for later.

Nutritional Information (Per Serving)
Calories: 180
Fats: 3g
Protein: 27g

Espresso-Cocoa Dusting Ice Cream

Time Needed to Prepare: 5 minutes
CREAMi Time: 3-4 minutes (including Mix-In function)
Number of Servings: 2

Ingredients List

- 1 cup of (240g) low-fat cottage cheese
- 1/2 cup of (120ml) unsweetened almond milk or skim milk
- 1 scoop (30g) chocolate or vanilla whey protein isolate
- 1 tablespoon of allulose or monk fruit sweetener
- 1/2 teaspoon vanilla extract
- 1/4 teaspoon xanthan gum
- 1 teaspoon unsweetened cocoa powder
- 1/2 teaspoon instant espresso powder

Instructions

1. In a blender, combine cottage cheese, almond milk, protein powder, sweetener, vanilla extract, and xanthan gum. Blend until completely smooth.
2. Pour the mixture into a Ninja CREAMi pint and secure the lid.
3. Freeze for 24 hours until solid.
4. Once frozen, place the pint into the Ninja CREAMi and lock it into the machine.
5. Select the "Lite Ice Cream" mode and process.
6. If the texture is too firm or crumbly, add 1-2 tablespoons of almond milk and press Re-Spin for extra creaminess.
7. In a small bowl, mix the cocoa powder and instant espresso powder.
8. Lightly dust the cocoa-espresso mixture over the ice cream before serving.
9. Serve immediately or store in the freezer with a lid for later.

Nutritional Information (Per Serving)
Calories: 185
Fats: 4g
Protein: 27g

CHAPTER 2: ICE CREAM MIX-INS

Crushed Protein Bar Chunks Ice Cream

Time Needed to Prepare: 5 minutes
CREAMi Time: 3-4 minutes (including Mix-In function)
Number of Servings: 2

Ingredients List

- 1 cup of (240g) low-fat cottage cheese
- 1/2 cup of (120ml) unsweetened almond milk or skim milk
- 1 scoop (30g) vanilla or chocolate whey protein isolate
- 1 tablespoon of allulose or monk fruit sweetener
- 1/2 teaspoon vanilla extract (or chocolate extract if using chocolate protein)
- 1/4 teaspoon xanthan gum
- 1 high-protein bar (low sugar, at least 15g protein), chopped into small chunks

Instructions

1. In a blender, combine cottage cheese, almond milk, protein powder, sweetener, vanilla extract, and xanthan gum. Blend until completely smooth.
2. Pour the mixture into a Ninja CREAMi pint and secure the lid.
3. Freeze for 24 hours until solid.
4. Once frozen, place the pint into the Ninja CREAMi and lock it into the machine.
5. Select the "Lite Ice Cream" mode and process.
6. If the texture is too firm or crumbly, add 1-2 tablespoons of almond milk and press Re-Spin for extra creaminess.
7. Create a small well in the center of the pint and add the chopped protein bar chunks.
8. Place the pint back into the Ninja CREAMi and select the "Mix-In" function.
9. Once mixed, serve immediately or store in the freezer with a lid for later.

Nutritional Information (Per Serving, Based on a 200-Calorie Protein Bar)
Calories: 210
Fats: 6g
Protein: 30g

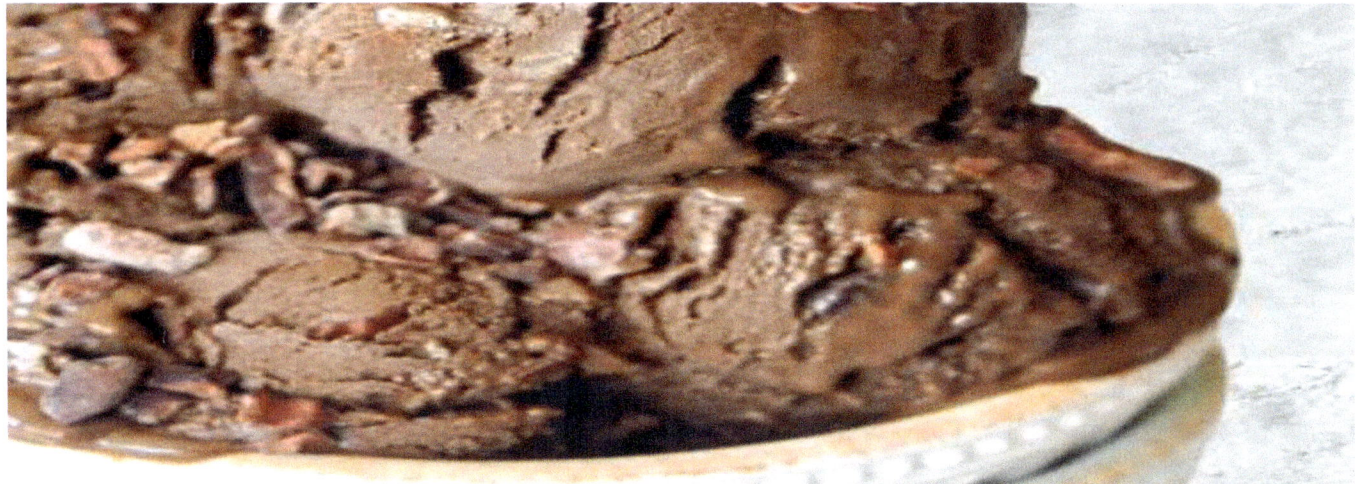

Sugar-Free Chocolate Chips & Cocoa Nibs Ice Cream

Time Needed to Prepare: 5 minutes
CREAMi Time: 3-4 minutes (including Mix-In function)
Number of Servings: 2

Ingredients List

- 1 cup of (240g) low-fat cottage cheese
- 1/2 cup of (120ml) unsweetened almond milk or skim milk
- 1 scoop (30g) chocolate or vanilla whey protein isolate
- 1 tablespoon of unsweetened cocoa powder (if using vanilla protein)
- 1 tablespoon of allulose or monk fruit sweetener
- 1/2 teaspoon vanilla extract
- 1/4 teaspoon xanthan gum
- 2 tablespoons of sugar-free chocolate chips
- 1 tablespoon of cocoa nibs

Instructions

1. In a blender, combine cottage cheese, almond milk, protein powder, cocoa powder (if using), sweetener, vanilla extract, and xanthan gum. Blend until completely smooth.
2. Pour the mixture into a Ninja CREAMi pint and secure the lid.
3. Freeze for 24 hours until solid.
4. Once frozen, place the pint into the Ninja CREAMi and lock it into the machine.
5. Select the "Lite Ice Cream" mode and process.
6. If the texture is too firm or crumbly, add 1-2 tablespoons of almond milk and press Re-Spin for extra creaminess.
7. Create a small well in the center of the pint and add the sugar-free chocolate chips and cocoa nibs.
8. Place the pint back into the Ninja CREAMi and select the "Mix-In" function.
9. Once mixed, serve immediately or store in the freezer with a lid for later.

Nutritional Information (Per Serving)
Calories: 200
Fats: 7g
Protein: 28g

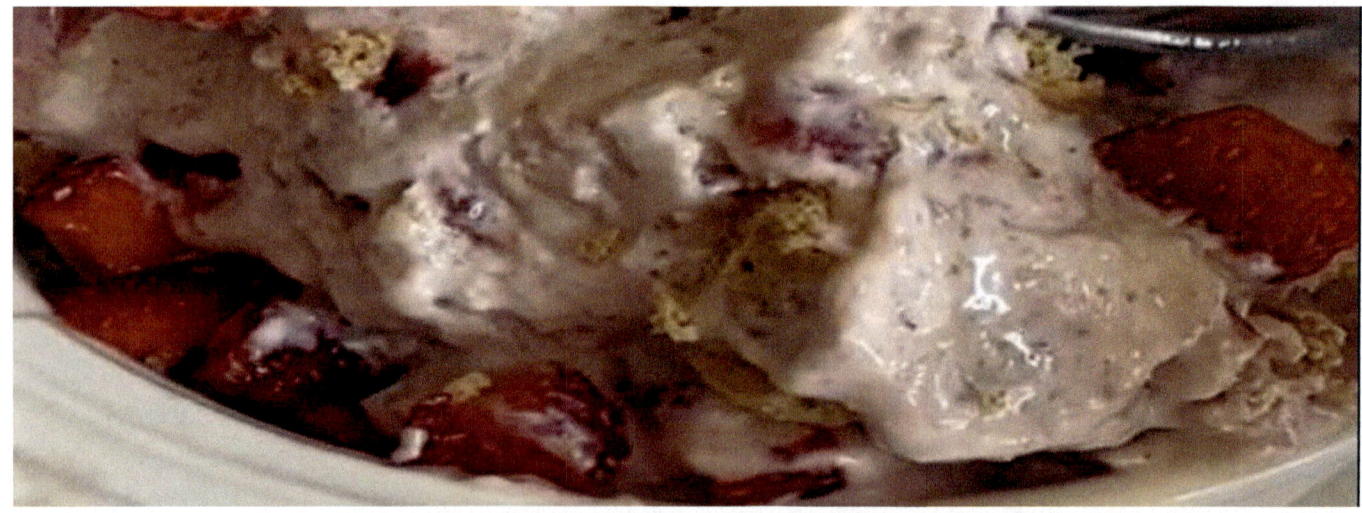

Strawberry Cheesecake Protein Ice Cream

Time Needed to Prepare: 5 minutes
CREAMi Time: 2-3 minutes (plus re-spin if needed)
Number of Servings: 2

Ingredients List

- 1 cup of (240g) low-fat cottage cheese
- 1/2 cup of (120ml) unsweetened almond milk or skim milk
- 1 scoop (30g) vanilla whey protein isolate
- 1/2 cup of (75g) fresh or frozen strawberries
- 1 tablespoon of sugar-free cheesecake pudding mix
- 1 tablespoon of allulose or monk fruit sweetener
- 1/2 teaspoon vanilla extract
- 1/4 teaspoon xanthan gum
- 1 crushed graham cracker (for mix-in)

Instructions

1. In a blender, combine cottage cheese, almond milk, protein powder, strawberries, cheesecake pudding mix, sweetener, vanilla extract, and xanthan gum. Blend until completely smooth.
2. Pour the mixture into a Ninja CREAMi pint and secure the lid.
3. Freeze for 24 hours until solid.
4. Once frozen, place the pint into the Ninja CREAMi and lock it into the machine.
5. Select the "Lite Ice Cream" mode and process.
6. If the texture is too firm or crumbly, add 1-2 tablespoons of almond milk and press Re-Spin for extra creaminess.
7. Once smooth, add the crushed graham cracker and press the 'Mix-In' button.
8. Serve immediately or store in the freezer with a lid for later.

Nutritional Information (Per Serving)
Calories: 195
Fats: 4g | **Protein:** 26g

Toasted Coconut & Almonds Ice Cream

Time Needed to Prepare: 5 minutes
CREAMi Time: 3-4 minutes (including Mix-In function)
Number of Servings: 2

Ingredients List

- 1 cup of (240g) low-fat cottage cheese
- 1/2 cup of (120ml) unsweetened almond milk or skim milk
- 1 scoop (30g) vanilla whey protein isolate
- 1 tablespoon of allulose or monk fruit sweetener
- 1/2 teaspoon vanilla extract
- 1/4 teaspoon xanthan gum
- 2 tablespoons of unsweetened shredded coconut, toasted
- 2 tablespoons of sliced almonds, toasted

Instructions

1. In a blender, combine cottage cheese, almond milk, protein powder, sweetener, vanilla extract, and xanthan gum. Blend until completely smooth.
2. Pour the mixture into a Ninja CREAMi pint and secure the lid.
3. Freeze for 24 hours until solid.
4. Once frozen, place the pint into the Ninja CREAMi and lock it into the machine.
5. Select the "Lite Ice Cream" mode and process.
6. If the texture is too firm or crumbly, add 1-2 tablespoons of almond milk and press Re-Spin for extra creaminess.
7. Create a small well in the center of the pint and add the toasted coconut and almonds.
8. Place the pint back into the Ninja CREAMi and select the "Mix-In" function.
9. Once mixed, serve immediately or store in the freezer with a lid for later.

Nutritional Information (Per Serving)
Calories: 210
Fats: 8g
Protein: 27g

Chia & Flax Seed Crunch Ice Cream

Time Needed to Prepare: 5 minutes
CREAMi Time: 3-4 minutes (including Mix-In function)
Number of Servings: 2

Ingredients List

- 1 cup of (240g) low-fat cottage cheese
- 1/2 cup of (120ml) unsweetened almond milk or skim milk
- 1 scoop (30g) vanilla whey protein isolate
- 1 tablespoon of allulose or monk fruit sweetener
- 1/2 teaspoon vanilla extract
- 1/4 teaspoon xanthan gum
- 1 tablespoon of chia seeds
- 1 tablespoon of ground flax seeds

Instructions

1. In a blender, combine cottage cheese, almond milk, protein powder, sweetener, vanilla extract, and xanthan gum. Blend until completely smooth.
2. Pour the mixture into a Ninja CREAMi pint and secure the lid.
3. Freeze for 24 hours until solid.
4. Once frozen, place the pint into the Ninja CREAMi and lock it into the machine.
5. Select the "Lite Ice Cream" mode and process.
6. If the texture is too firm or crumbly, add 1-2 tablespoons of almond milk and press Re-Spin for extra creaminess.
7. Create a small well in the center of the pint and add the chia seeds and ground flax seeds.
8. Place the pint back into the Ninja CREAMi and select the "Mix-In" function.
9. Once mixed, serve immediately or store in the freezer with a lid for later.

Nutritional Information (Per Serving)
Calories: 205
Fats: 7g | **Protein:** 27g

High-Protein Brownie Bites Ice Cream

Time Needed to Prepare: 5 minutes
CREAMi Time: 3-4 minutes (including Mix-In function)
Number of Servings: 2

Ingredients List

- 1 cup of (240g) low-fat cottage cheese
- 1/2 cup of (120ml) unsweetened almond milk or skim milk
- 1 scoop (30g) chocolate whey protein isolate
- 1 tablespoon of unsweetened cocoa powder
- 1 tablespoon of allulose or monk fruit sweetener
- 1/2 teaspoon vanilla extract
- 1/4 teaspoon xanthan gum
- 2 tablespoons of high-protein brownie bites (low sugar, at least 5g protein per serving)

Instructions

1. In a blender, combine cottage cheese, almond milk, protein powder, cocoa powder, sweetener, vanilla extract, and xanthan gum. Blend until completely smooth.
2. Pour the mixture into a Ninja CREAMi pint and secure the lid.
3. Freeze for 24 hours until solid.
4. Once frozen, place the pint into the Ninja CREAMi and lock it into the machine.
5. Select the "Lite Ice Cream" mode and process.
6. If the texture is too firm or crumbly, add 1-2 tablespoons of almond milk and press Re-Spin for extra creaminess.
7. Create a small well in the center of the pint and add the high-protein brownie bites.
8. Place the pint back into the Ninja CREAMi and select the "Mix-In" function.
9. Once mixed, serve immediately or store in the freezer with a lid for later.

Nutritional Information (Per Serving)
Calories: 215
Fats: 6g
Protein: 28g

Oatmeal Cookie Protein Crumbles Ice Cream

Time Needed to Prepare: 5 minutes
CREAMi Time: 3-4 minutes (including Mix-In function)
Number of Servings: 2

Ingredients List

- 1 cup of (240g) low-fat cottage cheese
- 1/2 cup of (120ml) unsweetened almond milk or skim milk
- 1 scoop (30g) vanilla whey protein isolate
- 1 tablespoon of allulose or monk fruit sweetener
- 1/2 teaspoon vanilla extract
- 1/4 teaspoon cinnamon
- 1/4 teaspoon xanthan gum
- 2 tablespoons of high-protein oatmeal cookie crumbles (low sugar, at least 5g protein per serving)

Instructions

1. In a blender, combine cottage cheese, almond milk, protein powder, sweetener, vanilla extract, cinnamon, and xanthan gum. Blend until completely smooth.
2. Pour the mixture into a Ninja CREAMi pint and secure the lid.
3. Freeze for 24 hours until solid.
4. Once frozen, place the pint into the Ninja CREAMi and lock it into the machine.
5. Select the "Lite Ice Cream" mode and process.
6. If the texture is too firm or crumbly, add 1-2 tablespoons of almond milk and press Re-Spin for extra creaminess.
7. Create a small well in the center of the pint and add the high-protein oatmeal cookie crumbles.
8. Place the pint back into the Ninja CREAMi and select the "Mix-In" function.
9. Once mixed, serve immediately or store in the freezer with a lid for later.

Nutritional Information (Per Serving)
Calories: 210
Fats: 5g
Protein: 27g

Collagen-Boosted Granola Clusters Ice Cream

Time Needed to Prepare: 5 minutes
CREAMi Time: 3-4 minutes (including Mix-In function)
Number of Servings: 2

Ingredients List

- 1 cup of (240g) low-fat cottage cheese
- 1/2 cup of (120ml) unsweetened almond milk or skim milk
- 1 scoop (30g) vanilla whey protein isolate
- 1 scoop (10g) unflavored collagen peptides
- 1 tablespoon of allulose or monk fruit sweetener
- 1/2 teaspoon vanilla extract
- 1/4 teaspoon xanthan gum
- 2 tablespoons of high-protein, low-sugar granola clusters

Instructions

1. In a blender, combine cottage cheese, almond milk, protein powder, collagen peptides, sweetener, vanilla extract, and xanthan gum. Blend until completely smooth.
2. Pour the mixture into a Ninja CREAMi pint and secure the lid.
3. Freeze for 24 hours until solid.
4. Once frozen, place the pint into the Ninja CREAMi and lock it into the machine.
5. Select the "Lite Ice Cream" mode and process.
6. If the texture is too firm or crumbly, add 1-2 tablespoons of almond milk and press Re-Spin for extra creaminess.
7. Create a small well in the center of the pint and add the high-protein granola clusters.
8. Place the pint back into the Ninja CREAMi and select the "Mix-In" function.
9. Once mixed, serve immediately or store in the freezer with a lid for later.

Nutritional Information (Per Serving)
Calories: 210
Fats: 5g
Protein: 30g

Cinnamon Toasted Pecans Ice Cream

Time Needed to Prepare: 5 minutes
CREAMi Time: 3-4 minutes (including Mix-In function)
Number of Servings: 2

Ingredients List

- 1 cup of (240g) low-fat cottage cheese
- 1/2 cup of (120ml) unsweetened almond milk or skim milk
- 1 scoop (30g) vanilla whey protein isolate
- 1 tablespoon of allulose or monk fruit sweetener
- 1/2 teaspoon vanilla extract
- 1/4 teaspoon xanthan gum
- 2 tablespoons of pecans, chopped
- 1/2 teaspoon ground cinnamon
- 1/2 teaspoon allulose or monk fruit sweetener (for pecans)

Instructions

1. In a small pan over medium heat, toast the chopped pecans for 2-3 minutes until fragrant.
2. Sprinkle with ground cinnamon and additional allulose, stirring to coat, then remove from heat and let cool.
3. In a blender, combine cottage cheese, almond milk, protein powder, sweetener, vanilla extract, and xanthan gum. Blend until completely smooth.
4. Pour the mixture into a Ninja CREAMi pint and secure the lid.
5. Freeze for 24 hours until solid.
6. Once frozen, place the pint into the Ninja CREAMi and lock it into the machine.
7. Select the "Lite Ice Cream" mode and process.
8. If the texture is too firm or crumbly, add 1-2 tablespoons of almond milk and press Re-Spin for extra creaminess.
9. Create a small well in the center of the pint and add the cinnamon-toasted pecans.
10. Place the pint back into the Ninja CREAMi and select the "Mix-In" function.
11. Once mixed, serve immediately or store in the freezer with a lid for later.

Nutritional Information (Per Serving)
Calories: 220
Fats: 7g | **Protein:** 28g

Sugar-Free Marshmallow Swirls Ice Cream

Time Needed to Prepare: 5 minutes
CREAMi Time: 3-4 minutes (including Mix-In function)
Number of Servings: 2

Ingredients List

- 1 cup of (240g) low-fat cottage cheese
- 1/2 cup of (120ml) unsweetened almond milk or skim milk
- 1 scoop (30g) vanilla whey protein isolate
- 1 tablespoon of allulose or monk fruit sweetener
- 1/2 teaspoon vanilla extract
- 1/4 teaspoon xanthan gum
- 2 tablespoons of sugar-free marshmallow fluff

Instructions

1. In a blender, combine cottage cheese, almond milk, protein powder, sweetener, vanilla extract, and xanthan gum. Blend until completely smooth.
2. Pour the mixture into a Ninja CREAMi pint and secure the lid.
3. Freeze for 24 hours until solid.
4. Once frozen, place the pint into the Ninja CREAMi and lock it into the machine.
5. Select the "Lite Ice Cream" mode and process.
6. If the texture is too firm or crumbly, add 1-2 tablespoons of almond milk and press Re-Spin for extra creaminess.
7. Create a small well in the center of the pint and add the sugar-free marshmallow fluff.
8. Place the pint back into the Ninja CREAMi and select the "Mix-In" function.
9. Once mixed, serve immediately or store in the freezer with a lid for later.

Nutritional Information (Per Serving)
Calories: 190
Fats: 3.5g | **Protein:** 27g

Crushed Freeze-Dried Berries Ice Cream

Time Needed to Prepare: 5 minutes
CREAMi Time: 3-4 minutes (including Mix-In function)
Number of Servings: 2

Ingredients List

- 1 cup of (240g) low-fat cottage cheese
- 1/2 cup of (120ml) unsweetened almond milk or skim milk
- 1 scoop (30g) vanilla whey protein isolate
- 1 tablespoon of allulose or monk fruit sweetener
- 1/2 teaspoon vanilla extract
- 1/4 teaspoon xanthan gum
- 2 tablespoons of crushed freeze-dried berries (strawberries, blueberries, or raspberries)

Instructions

1. In a blender, combine cottage cheese, almond milk, protein powder, sweetener, vanilla extract, and xanthan gum. Blend until completely smooth.
2. Pour the mixture into a Ninja CREAMi pint and secure the lid.
3. Freeze for 24 hours until solid.
4. Once frozen, place the pint into the Ninja CREAMi and lock it into the machine.
5. Select the "Lite Ice Cream" mode and process.
6. If the texture is too firm or crumbly, add 1-2 tablespoons of almond milk and press Re-Spin for extra creaminess.
7. Create a small well in the center of the pint and add the crushed freeze-dried berries.
8. Place the pint back into the Ninja CREAMi and select the "Mix-In" function.
9. Once mixed, serve immediately or store in the freezer with a lid for later.

Nutritional Information (Per Serving)
Calories: 190
Fats: 3.5g | **Protein:** 27g

CHAPTER 3: SMOOTHIE BOWL DELIGHTS

Tropical Mango Pineapple Protein Bowl

Time Needed to Prepare: 5 minutes
CREAMi Time: 3-4 minutes (plus Re-Spin if needed)
Number of Servings: 2

Ingredients List

- 1 cup of (240g) low-fat Greek yogurt
- 1/2 cup of (120ml) unsweetened coconut milk
- 1 scoop (30g) vanilla whey protein isolate
- 1/2 cup of (75g) frozen mango chunks
- 1/2 cup of (75g) frozen pineapple chunks
- 1 tablespoon of allulose or monk fruit sweetener
- 1/2 teaspoon vanilla extract
- 1/4 teaspoon xanthan gum
- 1 tablespoon of unsweetened shredded coconut (for topping)

Instructions

1. In a blender, combine Greek yogurt, coconut milk, protein powder, mango, pineapple, sweetener, vanilla extract, and xanthan gum. Blend until completely smooth.
2. Pour the mixture into a Ninja CREAMi pint and secure the lid.
3. Freeze for 24 hours until solid.
4. Once frozen, place the pint into the Ninja CREAMi and lock it into the machine.
5. Select the **"Smoothie Bowl"** mode and process.
6. If the texture is too firm or crumbly, add 1-2 tablespoons of coconut milk and press Re-Spin for extra creaminess.
7. Serve in a bowl and sprinkle with shredded coconut and any preferred topping before serving.
8. Enjoy immediately or store in the freezer with a lid for later.

Nutritional Information (Per Serving)
Calories: 210
Fats: 4g | **Protein:** 28g

Acai Superfood Protein Bowl

Time Needed to Prepare: 5 minutes
CREAMi Time: 3-4 minutes (plus Re-Spin if needed)
Number of Servings: 2

Ingredients List

- 1 cup of (240g) low-fat Greek yogurt
- 1/2 cup of (120ml) unsweetened almond milk
- 1 scoop (30g) vanilla or berry whey protein isolate
- 1/2 cup of (75g) frozen acai puree (unsweetened)
- 1/2 cup of (75g) frozen mixed berries (blueberries, raspberries, or strawberries)
- 1 tablespoon of allulose or monk fruit sweetener
- 1/2 teaspoon vanilla extract
- 1/4 teaspoon xanthan gum
- 1 tablespoon of chia seeds (for topping)

Instructions

1. In a blender, combine Greek yogurt, almond milk, protein powder, acai puree, mixed berries, sweetener, vanilla extract, and xanthan gum. Blend until completely smooth.
2. Pour the mixture into a Ninja CREAMi pint and secure the lid.
3. Freeze for 24 hours until solid.
4. Once frozen, place the pint into the Ninja CREAMi and lock it into the machine.
5. Select the **"Smoothie Bowl"** mode and process.
6. If the texture is too firm or crumbly, add 1-2 tablespoons of almond milk and press Re-Spin for extra creaminess.
7. Serve in a bowl and sprinkle with chia seeds and any preferred topping before serving.
8. Enjoy immediately or store in the freezer with a lid for later.

Nutritional Information (Per Serving)
Calories: 220
Fats: 5g
Protein: 29g

Chocolate Almond Butter Energy Bowl

Time Needed to Prepare: 5 minutes
CREAMi Time: 3-4 minutes (plus Re-Spin if needed)
Number of Servings: 2

Ingredients List

- 1 cup of (240g) low-fat Greek yogurt
- 1/2 cup of (120ml) unsweetened almond milk
- 1 scoop (30g) chocolate whey protein isolate
- 1 tablespoon of unsweetened cocoa powder
- 1 tablespoon of allulose or monk fruit sweetener
- 1 tablespoon of natural almond butter (no added sugar or oil)
- 1/2 teaspoon vanilla extract
- 1/4 teaspoon xanthan gum
- 1 tablespoon of chopped almonds (for topping)

Instructions

1. In a blender, combine Greek yogurt, almond milk, protein powder, cocoa powder, sweetener, almond butter, vanilla extract, and xanthan gum. Blend until completely smooth.
2. Pour the mixture into a Ninja CREAMi pint and secure the lid.
3. Freeze for 24 hours until solid.
4. Once frozen, place the pint into the Ninja CREAMi and lock it into the machine.
5. Select the **"Smoothie Bowl"** mode and process.
6. If the texture is too firm or crumbly, add 1-2 tablespoons of almond milk and press Re-Spin for extra creaminess.
7. Serve in a bowl and sprinkle with chopped almonds and any preferred topping before serving.
8. Enjoy immediately or store in the freezer with a lid for later.

Nutritional Information (Per Serving)
Calories: 235
Fats: 8g
Protein: 30g

Berry Blast Greek Yogurt Protein Bowl

Time Needed to Prepare: 5 minutes
CREAMi Time: 3-4 minutes (plus Re-Spin if needed)
Number of Servings: 2

Ingredients List

- 1 cup of (240g) low-fat Greek yogurt
- 1/2 cup of (120ml) unsweetened almond milk
- 1 scoop (30g) vanilla whey protein isolate
- 1/2 cup of (75g) frozen mixed berries (blueberries, raspberries, and strawberries)
- 1 tablespoon of allulose or monk fruit sweetener
- 1/2 teaspoon vanilla extract
- 1/4 teaspoon xanthan gum
- 1 tablespoon of fresh mixed berries (for topping)

Instructions

1. In a blender, combine Greek yogurt, almond milk, protein powder, frozen mixed berries, sweetener, vanilla extract, and xanthan gum. Blend until completely smooth.
2. Pour the mixture into a Ninja CREAMi pint and secure the lid.
3. Freeze for 24 hours until solid.
4. Once frozen, place the pint into the Ninja CREAMi and lock it into the machine.
5. Select the **"Smoothie Bowl"** mode and process.
6. If the texture is too firm or crumbly, add 1-2 tablespoons of almond milk and press Re-Spin for extra creaminess.
7. Serve in a bowl and top with fresh mixed berries before serving.
8. Enjoy immediately or store in the freezer with a lid for later.

Nutritional Information (Per Serving)
Calories: 210
Fats: 4g | **Protein:** 29g

Peanut Butter Banana Muscle Bowl

Time Needed to Prepare: 5 minutes
CREAMi Time: 3-4 minutes (plus Re-Spin if needed)
Number of Servings: 2

Ingredients List

- 1 cup of (240g) low-fat Greek yogurt
- 1/2 cup of (120ml) unsweetened almond milk
- 1 scoop (30g) vanilla or chocolate whey protein isolate
- 1 small ripe banana, sliced and frozen
- 1 tablespoon of natural peanut butter (no added sugar or oil)
- 1 tablespoon of allulose or monk fruit sweetener
- 1/2 teaspoon vanilla extract
- 1/4 teaspoon xanthan gum
- 1 tablespoon of crushed peanuts (for topping)

Instructions

1. In a blender, combine Greek yogurt, almond milk, protein powder, frozen banana, peanut butter, sweetener, vanilla extract, and xanthan gum. Blend until completely smooth.
2. Pour the mixture into a Ninja CREAMi pint and secure the lid.
3. Freeze for 24 hours until solid.
4. Once frozen, place the pint into the Ninja CREAMi and lock it into the machine.
5. Select the **"Smoothie Bowl"** mode and process.
6. If the texture is too firm or crumbly, add 1-2 tablespoons of almond milk and press Re-Spin for extra creaminess.
7. Serve in a bowl and top with crushed peanuts and any preferred topping before serving.
8. Enjoy immediately or store in the freezer with a lid for later.

Nutritional Information (Per Serving)
Calories: 230
Fats: 7g | **Protein:** 30g

Green Machine Spinach Protein Bowl

Time Needed to Prepare: 5 minutes
CREAMi Time: 3-4 minutes (plus Re-Spin if needed)
Number of Servings: 2

Ingredients List

- 1 cup of (240g) low-fat Greek yogurt
- 1/2 cup of (120ml) unsweetened almond milk
- 1 scoop (30g) vanilla whey protein isolate
- 1/2 cup of (30g) fresh spinach, packed
- 1/2 frozen banana
- 1 tablespoon of allulose or monk fruit sweetener
- 1/2 teaspoon vanilla extract
- 1/4 teaspoon xanthan gum
- 1 tablespoon of chia seeds (for topping)

Instructions

1. In a blender, combine Greek yogurt, almond milk, protein powder, spinach, frozen banana, sweetener, vanilla extract, and xanthan gum. Blend until completely smooth.
2. Pour the mixture into a Ninja CREAMi pint and secure the lid.
3. Freeze for 24 hours until solid.
4. Once frozen, place the pint into the Ninja CREAMi and lock it into the machine.
5. Select the **"Smoothie Bowl"** mode and process.
6. If the texture is too firm or crumbly, add 1-2 tablespoons of almond milk and press Re-Spin for extra creaminess.
7. Serve in a bowl and top with chia seeds and any preferred topping before serving.
8. Enjoy immediately or store in the freezer with a lid for later.

Nutritional Information (Per Serving)
Calories: 200
Fats: 4g
Protein: 29g

Vanilla Coconut Crunch Smoothie Bowl

Time Needed to Prepare: 5 minutes
CREAMi Time: 3-4 minutes (plus Re-Spin if needed)
Number of Servings: 2

Ingredients List

- 1 cup of (240g) low-fat Greek yogurt
- 1/2 cup of (120ml) unsweetened coconut milk
- 1 scoop (30g) vanilla whey protein isolate
- 1 tablespoon of allulose or monk fruit sweetener
- 1/2 teaspoon vanilla extract
- 1/4 teaspoon xanthan gum
- 2 tablespoons of unsweetened shredded coconut
- 1 tablespoon of crushed almonds (for topping)

Instructions

1. In a blender, combine Greek yogurt, coconut milk, protein powder, sweetener, vanilla extract, and xanthan gum. Blend until completely smooth.
2. Pour the mixture into a Ninja CREAMi pint and secure the lid.
3. Freeze for 24 hours until solid.
4. Once frozen, place the pint into the Ninja CREAMi and lock it into the machine.
5. Select the **"Smoothie Bowl"** mode and process.
6. If the texture is too firm or crumbly, add 1-2 tablespoons of coconut milk and press Re-Spin for extra creaminess.
7. Serve in a bowl and top with shredded coconut and crushed almonds before serving.
8. Enjoy immediately or store in the freezer with a lid for later.

Nutritional Information (Per Serving)
Calories: 220
Fats: 7g
Protein: 30g

Mocha Oatmeal Protein Bowl

Time Needed to Prepare: 5 minutes
CREAMi Time: 3-4 minutes (plus Re-Spin if needed)
Number of Servings: 2

Ingredients List

- 1 cup of (240g) low-fat Greek yogurt
- 1/2 cup of (120ml) unsweetened almond milk
- 1 scoop (30g) chocolate whey protein isolate
- 1 tablespoon of unsweetened cocoa powder
- 1 teaspoon instant espresso powder
- 1/4 cup of (20g) rolled oats
- 1 tablespoon of allulose or monk fruit sweetener
- 1/2 teaspoon vanilla extract
- 1/4 teaspoon xanthan gum
- 1 tablespoon of cacao nibs (for topping)

Instructions

1. In a blender, combine Greek yogurt, almond milk, protein powder, cocoa powder, espresso powder, oats, sweetener, vanilla extract, and xanthan gum. Blend until completely smooth.
2. Pour the mixture into a Ninja CREAMi pint and secure the lid.
3. Freeze for 24 hours until solid.
4. Once frozen, place the pint into the Ninja CREAMi and lock it into the machine.
5. Select the **"Smoothie Bowl"** mode and process.
6. If the texture is too firm or crumbly, add 1-2 tablespoons of almond milk and press Re-Spin for extra creaminess.
7. Serve in a bowl and top with cacao nibs before serving.
8. Enjoy immediately or store in the freezer with a lid for later.

Nutritional Information (Per Serving)
Calories: 230
Fats: 5g
Protein: 29g

Strawberry Kiwi Power Bowl

Time Needed to Prepare: 5 minutes
CREAMi Time: 3-4 minutes (plus Re-Spin if needed)
Number of Servings: 2

Ingredients List

- 1 cup of (240g) low-fat Greek yogurt
- 1/2 cup of (120ml) unsweetened almond milk
- 1 scoop (30g) vanilla whey protein isolate
- 1/2 cup of (75g) frozen strawberries
- 1 medium kiwi, peeled and chopped
- 1 tablespoon of allulose or monk fruit sweetener
- 1/2 teaspoon vanilla extract
- 1/4 teaspoon xanthan gum
- 1 tablespoon of chia seeds (for topping)

Instructions

1. In a blender, combine Greek yogurt, almond milk, protein powder, strawberries, kiwi, sweetener, vanilla extract, and xanthan gum. Blend until completely smooth.
2. Pour the mixture into a Ninja CREAMi pint and secure the lid.
3. Freeze for 24 hours until solid.
4. Once frozen, place the pint into the Ninja CREAMi and lock it into the machine.
5. Select the **"Smoothie Bowl"** mode and process.
6. If the texture is too firm or crumbly, add 1-2 tablespoons of almond milk and press Re-Spin for extra creaminess.
7. Serve in a bowl and top with chia seeds before serving.
8. Enjoy immediately or store in the freezer with a lid for later.

Nutritional Information (Per Serving)
Calories: 215
Fats: 4g
Protein: 29g

Blueberry Vanilla Whey Bowl

Time Needed to Prepare: 5 minutes
CREAMi Time: 3-4 minutes (plus Re-Spin if needed)
Number of Servings: 2

Ingredients List

- 1 cup of (240g) low-fat Greek yogurt
- 1/2 cup of (120ml) unsweetened almond milk
- 1 scoop (30g) vanilla whey protein isolate
- 1/2 cup of (75g) frozen blueberries
- 1 tablespoon of allulose or monk fruit sweetener
- 1/2 teaspoon vanilla extract
- 1/4 teaspoon xanthan gum
- 1 tablespoon of crushed walnuts (for topping)

Instructions

1. In a blender, combine Greek yogurt, almond milk, protein powder, blueberries, sweetener, vanilla extract, and xanthan gum. Blend until completely smooth.
2. Pour the mixture into a Ninja CREAMi pint and secure the lid.
3. Freeze for 24 hours until solid.
4. Once frozen, place the pint into the Ninja CREAMi and lock it into the machine.
5. Select the **"Smoothie Bowl"** mode and process.
6. If the texture is too firm or crumbly, add 1-2 tablespoons of almond milk and press Re-Spin for extra creaminess.
7. Serve in a bowl and top with crushed walnuts before serving.
8. Enjoy immediately or store in the freezer with a lid for later.

Nutritional Information (Per Serving)
Calories: 220
Fats: 5g
Protein: 30g

Apple Pie Cinnamon Protein Bowl

Time Needed to Prepare: 5 minutes
CREAMi Time: 3-4 minutes (plus Re-Spin if needed)
Number of Servings: 2

Ingredients List

- 1 cup of (240g) low-fat Greek yogurt
- 1/2 cup of (120ml) unsweetened almond milk
- 1 scoop (30g) vanilla whey protein isolate
- 1/2 cup of (75g) unsweetened applesauce
- 1/2 teaspoon ground cinnamon
- 1 tablespoon of allulose or monk fruit sweetener
- 1/2 teaspoon vanilla extract
- 1/4 teaspoon xanthan gum
- 1 tablespoon of crushed walnuts (for topping)

Instructions

1. In a blender, combine Greek yogurt, almond milk, protein powder, applesauce, cinnamon, sweetener, vanilla extract, and xanthan gum. Blend until completely smooth.
2. Pour the mixture into a Ninja CREAMi pint and secure the lid.
3. Freeze for 24 hours until solid.
4. Once frozen, place the pint into the Ninja CREAMi and lock it into the machine.
5. Select the **"Smoothie Bowl"** mode and process.
6. If the texture is too firm or crumbly, add 1-2 tablespoons of almond milk and press Re-Spin for extra creaminess.
7. Serve in a bowl and top with crushed walnuts before serving.
8. Enjoy immediately or store in the freezer with a lid for later.

Nutritional Information (Per Serving)
Calories: 225
Fats: 6g
Protein: 30g

CHAPTER 4: GELATO

Italian Vanilla Bean Whey Gelato

Time Needed to Prepare: 5 minutes
CREAMi Time: 3-4 minutes (plus Re-Spin if needed)
Number of Servings: 2

Ingredients List

- 1 cup of (240g) low-fat cottage cheese
- 1/2 cup of (120ml) unsweetened almond milk or skim milk
- 1 scoop (30g) vanilla whey protein isolate
- 1 tablespoon of sugar-free vanilla pudding mix
- 1 tablespoon of allulose or monk fruit sweetener
- 1 teaspoon vanilla bean paste or pure vanilla extract
- 1/4 teaspoon xanthan gum

Instructions

1. In a blender, combine cottage cheese, almond milk, protein powder, pudding mix, sweetener, vanilla bean paste, and xanthan gum. Blend until completely smooth.
2. Pour the mixture into a Ninja CREAMi pint and secure the lid.
3. Freeze for 24 hours until solid.
4. Once frozen, place the pint into the Ninja CREAMi and lock it into the machine.
5. Select the **"Gelato"** mode and process.
6. If the texture is too firm or crumbly, add 1-2 tablespoons of almond milk and press Re-Spin for extra creaminess.
7. Serve immediately or store in the freezer with a lid for later.

Nutritional Information (Per Serving)
Calories: 190
Fats: 4g | **Protein:** 28g

Dark Chocolate Hazelnut Protein Gelato

Time Needed to Prepare: 5 minutes
CREAMi Time: 3-4 minutes (plus Re-Spin if needed)
Number of Servings: 2

Ingredients List

- 1 cup of (240g) low-fat cottage cheese
- 1/2 cup of (120ml) unsweetened almond milk or skim milk
- 1 scoop (30g) chocolate whey protein isolate
- 1 tablespoon of unsweetened cocoa powder
- 1 tablespoon of allulose or monk fruit sweetener
- 1 teaspoon sugar-free hazelnut extract
- 1/4 teaspoon xanthan gum
- 1 tablespoon of crushed toasted hazelnuts (for topping)

Instructions

1. In a blender, combine cottage cheese, almond milk, protein powder, cocoa powder, sweetener, hazelnut extract, and xanthan gum. Blend until completely smooth.
2. Pour the mixture into a Ninja CREAMi pint and secure the lid.
3. Freeze for 24 hours until solid.
4. Once frozen, place the pint into the Ninja CREAMi and lock it into the machine.
5. Select the **"Gelato"** mode and process.
6. If the texture is too firm or crumbly, add 1-2 tablespoons of almond milk and press Re-Spin for extra creaminess.
7. Serve immediately, topped with crushed toasted hazelnuts, or store in the freezer with a lid for later.

Nutritional Information (Per Serving)
Calories: 200
Fats: 5g
Protein: 29g

Pistachio Almond Cream Gelato

Time Needed to Prepare: 5 minutes
CREAMi Time: 3-4 minutes (plus Re-Spin if needed)
Number of Servings: 2

Ingredients List

- 1 cup of (240g) low-fat cottage cheese
- 1/2 cup of (120ml) unsweetened almond milk or skim milk
- 1 scoop (30g) vanilla whey protein isolate
- 1 tablespoon of sugar-free pistachio pudding mix
- 1 tablespoon of allulose or monk fruit sweetener
- 1/2 teaspoon almond extract
- 1/4 teaspoon xanthan gum
- 1 tablespoon of crushed toasted pistachios (for topping)

Instructions

1. In a blender, combine cottage cheese, almond milk, protein powder, pistachio pudding mix, sweetener, almond extract, and xanthan gum. Blend until completely smooth.
2. Pour the mixture into a Ninja CREAMi pint and secure the lid.
3. Freeze for 24 hours until solid.
4. Once frozen, place the pint into the Ninja CREAMi and lock it into the machine.
5. Select the **"Gelato"** mode and process.
6. If the texture is too firm or crumbly, add 1-2 tablespoons of almond milk and press Re-Spin for extra creaminess.
7. Serve immediately, topped with crushed toasted pistachios, or store in the freezer with a lid for later.

Nutritional Information (Per Serving)
Calories: 205
Fats: 6g
Protein: 28g

Espresso Macchiato Protein Gelato

Time Needed to Prepare: 5 minutes
CREAMi Time: 3-4 minutes (plus Re-Spin if needed)
Number of Servings: 2

Ingredients List

- 1 cup of (240g) low-fat cottage cheese
- 1/2 cup of (120ml) unsweetened almond milk or skim milk
- 1 scoop (30g) vanilla whey protein isolate
- 1 teaspoon instant espresso powder
- 1 tablespoon of allulose or monk fruit sweetener
- 1/2 teaspoon vanilla extract
- 1/4 teaspoon xanthan gum
- 1 teaspoon sugar-free caramel drizzle (for topping)

Instructions

1. In a blender, combine cottage cheese, almond milk, protein powder, espresso powder, sweetener, vanilla extract, and xanthan gum. Blend until completely smooth.
2. Pour the mixture into a Ninja CREAMi pint and secure the lid.
3. Freeze for 24 hours until solid.
4. Once frozen, place the pint into the Ninja CREAMi and lock it into the machine.
5. Select the **"Gelato"** mode and process.
6. If the texture is too firm or crumbly, add 1-2 tablespoons of almond milk and press Re-Spin for extra creaminess.
7. Serve immediately, topped with sugar-free caramel drizzle, or store in the freezer with a lid for later.

Nutritional Information (Per Serving)
Calories: 190
Fats: 4g | **Protein:** 28g

Coconut Cashew High-Protein Gelato

Time Needed to Prepare: 5 minutes
CREAMi Time: 3-4 minutes (plus Re-Spin if needed)
Number of Servings: 2

Ingredients List

- 1 cup of (240g) low-fat cottage cheese
- 1/2 cup of (120ml) unsweetened coconut milk
- 1 scoop (30g) vanilla whey protein isolate
- 1 tablespoon of unsweetened shredded coconut
- 1 tablespoon of allulose or monk fruit sweetener
- 1/2 teaspoon vanilla extract
- 1/4 teaspoon xanthan gum
- 1 tablespoon of crushed roasted cashews (for topping)

Instructions

1. In a blender, combine cottage cheese, coconut milk, protein powder, shredded coconut, sweetener, vanilla extract, and xanthan gum. Blend until completely smooth.
2. Pour the mixture into a Ninja CREAMi pint and secure the lid.
3. Freeze for 24 hours until solid.
4. Once frozen, place the pint into the Ninja CREAMi and lock it into the machine.
5. Select the **"Gelato"** mode and process.
6. If the texture is too firm or crumbly, add 1-2 tablespoons of coconut milk and press Re-Spin for extra creaminess.
7. Serve immediately, topped with crushed roasted cashews, or store in the freezer with a lid for later.

Nutritional Information (Per Serving)
Calories: 210
Fats: 6g | **Protein:** 28g

Tiramisu Collagen-Boosted Gelato

Time Needed to Prepare: 5 minutes
CREAMi Time: 3-4 minutes (plus Re-Spin if needed)
Number of Servings: 2

Ingredients List

- 1 cup of (240g) low-fat cottage cheese
- 1/2 cup of (120ml) unsweetened almond milk or skim milk
- 1 scoop (30g) vanilla whey protein isolate
- 1 scoop (10g) unflavored collagen peptides
- 1 teaspoon instant espresso powder
- 1 tablespoon of allulose or monk fruit sweetener
- 1/2 teaspoon vanilla extract
- 1/4 teaspoon xanthan gum
- 1/2 teaspoon unsweetened cocoa powder (for topping)

Instructions

1. In a blender, combine cottage cheese, almond milk, protein powder, collagen peptides, espresso powder, sweetener, vanilla extract, and xanthan gum. Blend until completely smooth.
2. Pour the mixture into a Ninja CREAMi pint and secure the lid.
3. Freeze for 24 hours until solid.
4. Once frozen, place the pint into the Ninja CREAMi and lock it into the machine.
5. Select the **"Gelato"** mode and process.
6. If the texture is too firm or crumbly, add 1-2 tablespoons of almond milk and press Re-Spin for extra creaminess.
7. Serve immediately, dusted with unsweetened cocoa powder, or store in the freezer with a lid for later.

Nutritional Information (Per Serving)
Calories: 195
Fats: 4g
Protein: 30g

Raspberry Chocolate Swirl Protein Gelato

Time Needed to Prepare: 5 minutes
CREAMi Time: 3-4 minutes (plus Re-Spin if needed)
Number of Servings: 2

Ingredients List

- 1 cup of (240g) low-fat cottage cheese
- 1/2 cup of (120ml) unsweetened almond milk or skim milk
- 1 scoop (30g) chocolate whey protein isolate
- 1/2 cup of (75g) frozen raspberries
- 1 tablespoon of allulose or monk fruit sweetener
- 1/2 teaspoon vanilla extract
- 1/4 teaspoon xanthan gum
- 1 teaspoon sugar-free chocolate syrup (for swirl)

Instructions

1. In a blender, combine cottage cheese, almond milk, protein powder, raspberries, sweetener, vanilla extract, and xanthan gum. Blend until completely smooth.
2. Pour the mixture into a Ninja CREAMi pint and secure the lid.
3. Freeze for 24 hours until solid.
4. Once frozen, place the pint into the Ninja CREAMi and lock it into the machine.
5. Select the **"Gelato"** mode and process.
6. If the texture is too firm or crumbly, add 1-2 tablespoons of almond milk and press Re-Spin for extra creaminess.
7. Drizzle the sugar-free chocolate syrup over the gelato and use a spoon to gently swirl it in before serving.
8. Serve immediately or store in the freezer with a lid for later.

Nutritional Information (Per Serving)
Calories: 200
Fats: 4.5g | **Protein:** 28g

Honey Lavender Protein Gelato

Time Needed to Prepare: 5 minutes
CREAMi Time: 3-4 minutes (plus Re-Spin if needed)
Number of Servings: 2

Ingredients List

- 1 cup of (240g) low-fat cottage cheese
- 1/2 cup of (120ml) unsweetened almond milk or skim milk
- 1 scoop (30g) vanilla whey protein isolate
- 1 tablespoon of allulose or monk fruit sweetener
- 1 teaspoon raw honey
- 1/2 teaspoon dried culinary lavender
- 1/2 teaspoon vanilla extract
- 1/4 teaspoon xanthan gum

Instructions

1. In a blender, combine cottage cheese, almond milk, protein powder, sweetener, honey, lavender, vanilla extract, and xanthan gum. Blend until completely smooth.
2. Pour the mixture into a Ninja CREAMi pint and secure the lid.
3. Freeze for 24 hours until solid.
4. Once frozen, place the pint into the Ninja CREAMi and lock it into the machine.
5. Select the **"Gelato"** mode and process.
6. If the texture is too firm or crumbly, add 1-2 tablespoons of almond milk and press Re-Spin for extra creaminess.
7. Serve immediately or store in the freezer with a lid for later.

Nutritional Information (Per Serving)
Calories: 195
Fats: 4g
Protein: 28g

Lemon Ricotta Whey Gelato

Time Needed to Prepare: 5 minutes
CREAMi Time: 3-4 minutes (plus Re-Spin if needed)
Number of Servings: 2

Ingredients List

- 1 cup of (240g) low-fat ricotta cheese
- 1/2 cup of (120ml) unsweetened almond milk or skim milk
- 1 scoop (30g) vanilla whey protein isolate
- 1 tablespoon of allulose or monk fruit sweetener
- 1 teaspoon fresh lemon zest
- 1 teaspoon fresh lemon juice
- 1/2 teaspoon vanilla extract
- 1/4 teaspoon xanthan gum

Instructions

1. In a blender, combine ricotta cheese, almond milk, protein powder, sweetener, lemon zest, lemon juice, vanilla extract, and xanthan gum. Blend until completely smooth.
2. Pour the mixture into a Ninja CREAMi pint and secure the lid.
3. Freeze for 24 hours until solid.
4. Once frozen, place the pint into the Ninja CREAMi and lock it into the machine.
5. Select the **"Gelato"** mode and process.
6. If the texture is too firm or crumbly, add 1-2 tablespoons of almond milk and press Re-Spin for extra creaminess.
7. Serve immediately or store in the freezer with a lid for later.

Nutritional Information (Per Serving)
Calories: 205
Fats: 5g
Protein: 28g

Maple Walnut High-Protein Gelato

Time Needed to Prepare: 5 minutes
CREAMi Time: 3-4 minutes (plus Re-Spin if needed)
Number of Servings: 2

Ingredients List

- 1 cup of (240g) low-fat cottage cheese
- 1/2 cup of (120ml) unsweetened almond milk or skim milk
- 1 scoop (30g) vanilla whey protein isolate
- 1 tablespoon of sugar-free maple syrup
- 1 tablespoon of allulose or monk fruit sweetener
- 1/2 teaspoon vanilla extract
- 1/4 teaspoon xanthan gum
- 2 tablespoons of chopped toasted walnuts (for topping)

Instructions

1. In a blender, combine cottage cheese, almond milk, protein powder, sugar-free maple syrup, sweetener, vanilla extract, and xanthan gum. Blend until completely smooth.
2. Pour the mixture into a Ninja CREAMi pint and secure the lid.
3. Freeze for 24 hours until solid.
4. Once frozen, place the pint into the Ninja CREAMi and lock it into the machine.
5. Select the **"Gelato"** mode and process.
6. If the texture is too firm or crumbly, add 1-2 tablespoons of almond milk and press Re-Spin for extra creaminess.
7. Serve immediately, topped with chopped toasted walnuts, or store in the freezer with a lid for later.

Nutritional Information (Per Serving)
Calories: 215
Fats: 6g | **Protein:** 28g

Chai Spice Protein Gelato

Time Needed to Prepare: 5 minutes
CREAMi Time: 3-4 minutes (plus Re-Spin if needed)
Number of Servings: 2

Ingredients List

- 1 cup of (240g) low-fat cottage cheese
- 1/2 cup of (120ml) unsweetened almond milk or skim milk
- 1 scoop (30g) vanilla whey protein isolate
- 1 tablespoon of allulose or monk fruit sweetener
- 1/2 teaspoon vanilla extract
- 1/2 teaspoon ground cinnamon
- 1/4 teaspoon ground ginger
- 1/4 teaspoon ground cardamom
- 1/8 teaspoon ground cloves
- 1/8 teaspoon ground nutmeg
- 1/4 teaspoon xanthan gum

Instructions

1. In a blender, combine cottage cheese, almond milk, protein powder, sweetener, vanilla extract, cinnamon, ginger, cardamom, cloves, nutmeg, and xanthan gum. Blend until completely smooth.
2. Pour the mixture into a Ninja CREAMi pint and secure the lid.
3. Freeze for 24 hours until solid.
4. Once frozen, place the pint into the Ninja CREAMi and lock it into the machine.
5. Select the **"Gelato"** mode and process.
6. If the texture is too firm or crumbly, add 1-2 tablespoons of almond milk and press Re-Spin for extra creaminess.
7. Serve immediately or store in the freezer with a lid for later.

Nutritional Information (Per Serving)
Calories: 200
Fats: 4g | **Protein:** 28g

Black Sesame Whey Gelato

Time Needed to Prepare: 5 minutes
CREAMi Time: 3-4 minutes (plus Re-Spin if needed)
Number of Servings: 2

Ingredients List

- 1 cup of (240g) low-fat cottage cheese
- 1/2 cup of (120ml) unsweetened almond milk or skim milk
- 1 scoop (30g) vanilla whey protein isolate
- 1 tablespoon of black sesame paste (unsweetened)
- 1 tablespoon of allulose or monk fruit sweetener
- 1/2 teaspoon vanilla extract
- 1/4 teaspoon xanthan gum
- 1 teaspoon toasted black sesame seeds (for topping)

Instructions

1. In a blender, combine cottage cheese, almond milk, protein powder, black sesame paste, sweetener, vanilla extract, and xanthan gum. Blend until completely smooth.
2. Pour the mixture into a Ninja CREAMi pint and secure the lid.
3. Freeze for 24 hours until solid.
4. Once frozen, place the pint into the Ninja CREAMi and lock it into the machine.
5. Select the **"Gelato"** mode and process.
6. If the texture is too firm or crumbly, add 1-2 tablespoons of almond milk and press Re-Spin for extra creaminess.
7. Serve immediately, topped with toasted black sesame seeds, or store in the freezer with a lid for later.

Nutritional Information (Per Serving)
Calories: 210
Fats: 6g
Protein: 28g

CHAPTER 5: SORBETS

Pineapple Ginger Recovery Sorbet

Time Needed to Prepare: 5 minutes
CREAMi Time: 3-4 minutes (plus Re-Spin if needed)
Number of Servings: 2

Ingredients List

- 1 cup of (150g) frozen pineapple chunks
- 1/2 cup of (120ml) unsweetened coconut water
- 1 scoop (30g) unflavored or vanilla whey protein isolate
- 1 tablespoon of allulose or monk fruit sweetener
- 1/2 teaspoon fresh grated ginger
- 1/2 teaspoon lime juice

Instructions

1. In a blender, combine frozen pineapple, coconut water, protein powder, sweetener, grated ginger, and lime juice. Blend until smooth.
2. Pour the mixture into a Ninja CREAMi pint and secure the lid.
3. Freeze for 24 hours until solid.
4. Once frozen, place the pint into the Ninja CREAMi and lock it into the machine.
5. Select the **"Sorbet"** mode and process.
6. If the texture is too firm or crumbly, add 1-2 tablespoons of coconut water and press Re-Spin for extra smoothness.
7. Serve immediately or store in the freezer with a lid for later.

Nutritional Information (Per Serving)
Calories: 160
Fats: 0.5g
Protein: 25g

Raspberry Lemonade Whey Sorbet

Time Needed to Prepare: 5 minutes
CREAMi Time: 3-4 minutes (plus Re-Spin if needed)
Number of Servings: 2

Ingredients List

- 1 cup of (150g) frozen raspberries
- 1/2 cup of (120ml) unsweetened lemonade
- 1 scoop (30g) unflavored or vanilla whey protein isolate
- 1 tablespoon of allulose or monk fruit sweetener
- 1/2 teaspoon lemon zest
- 1/2 teaspoon fresh lemon juice

Instructions

1. In a blender, combine frozen raspberries, lemonade, protein powder, sweetener, lemon zest, and lemon juice. Blend until smooth.
2. Pour the mixture into a Ninja CREAMi pint and secure the lid.
3. Freeze for 24 hours until solid.
4. Once frozen, place the pint into the Ninja CREAMi and lock it into the machine.
5. Select the **"Sorbet"** mode and process.
6. If the texture is too firm or crumbly, add 1-2 tablespoons of lemonade and press Re-Spin for extra smoothness.
7. Serve immediately or store in the freezer with a lid for later.

Nutritional Information (Per Serving)
Calories: 150
Fats: 0.5g
Protein: 24g

Watermelon Mint Electrolyte Sorbet

Time Needed to Prepare: 5 minutes
CREAMi Time: 3-4 minutes (plus Re-Spin if needed)
Number of Servings: 2

Ingredients List

- 1 cup of (150g) frozen watermelon chunks
- 1/2 cup of (120ml) unsweetened coconut water
- 1 scoop (30g) unflavored or watermelon-flavored whey protein isolate
- 1 tablespoon of allulose or monk fruit sweetener
- 4-5 fresh mint leaves
- 1/2 teaspoon lime juice

Instructions

1. In a blender, combine frozen watermelon, coconut water, protein powder, sweetener, mint leaves, and lime juice. Blend until smooth.
2. Pour the mixture into a Ninja CREAMi pint and secure the lid.
3. Freeze for 24 hours until solid.
4. Once frozen, place the pint into the Ninja CREAMi and lock it into the machine.
5. Select the **"Sorbet"** mode and process.
6. If the texture is too firm or crumbly, add 1-2 tablespoons of coconut water and press Re-Spin for extra smoothness.
7. Serve immediately or store in the freezer with a lid for later.

Nutritional Information (Per Serving)
Calories: 145
Fats: 0g
Protein: 24g

Peach Mango Collagen Sorbet

Time Needed to Prepare: 5 minutes
CREAMi Time: 3-4 minutes (plus Re-Spin if needed)
Number of Servings: 2

Ingredients List

- 1 cup of (150g) frozen peach slices
- 1/2 cup of (120ml) unsweetened mango juice
- 1 scoop (10g) unflavored collagen peptides
- 1 scoop (30g) unflavored or vanilla whey protein isolate
- 1 tablespoon of allulose or monk fruit sweetener
- 1/2 teaspoon lime juice

Instructions

1. In a blender, combine frozen peaches, mango juice, collagen peptides, protein powder, sweetener, and lime juice. Blend until smooth.
2. Pour the mixture into a Ninja CREAMi pint and secure the lid.
3. Freeze for 24 hours until solid.
4. Once frozen, place the pint into the Ninja CREAMi and lock it into the machine.
5. Select the **"Sorbet"** mode and process.
6. If the texture is too firm or crumbly, add 1-2 tablespoons of mango juice and press Re-Spin for extra smoothness.
7. Serve immediately or store in the freezer with a lid for later.

Nutritional Information (Per Serving)
Calories: 155
Fats: 0.5g
Protein: 25g

Strawberry Basil High-Protein Sorbet

Time Needed to Prepare: 5 minutes
CREAMi Time: 3-4 minutes (plus Re-Spin if needed)
Number of Servings: 2

Ingredients List

- 1 cup of (150g) frozen strawberries
- 1/2 cup of (120ml) unsweetened coconut water
- 1 scoop (30g) unflavored or vanilla whey protein isolate
- 1 tablespoon of allulose or monk fruit sweetener
- 3-4 fresh basil leaves
- 1/2 teaspoon lemon juice

Instructions

1. In a blender, combine frozen strawberries, coconut water, protein powder, sweetener, basil leaves, and lemon juice. Blend until smooth.
2. Pour the mixture into a Ninja CREAMi pint and secure the lid.
3. Freeze for 24 hours until solid.
4. Once frozen, place the pint into the Ninja CREAMi and lock it into the machine.
5. Select the **"Sorbet"** mode and process.
6. If the texture is too firm or crumbly, add 1-2 tablespoons of coconut water and press Re-Spin for extra smoothness.
7. Serve immediately or store in the freezer with a lid for later.

Nutritional Information (Per Serving)
Calories: 150
Fats: 0g
Protein: 24g

Blueberry Acai Superfood Sorbet

Time Needed to Prepare: 5 minutes
CREAMi Time: 3-4 minutes (plus Re-Spin if needed)
Number of Servings: 2

Ingredients List

- 1 cup of (150g) frozen blueberries
- 1/2 cup of (120ml) unsweetened acai juice
- 1 scoop (30g) unflavored or vanilla whey protein isolate
- 1 tablespoon of allulose or monk fruit sweetener
- 1/2 teaspoon lemon juice

Instructions

1. In a blender, combine frozen blueberries, acai juice, protein powder, sweetener, and lemon juice. Blend until smooth.
2. Pour the mixture into a Ninja CREAMi pint and secure the lid.
3. Freeze for 24 hours until solid.
4. Once frozen, place the pint into the Ninja CREAMi and lock it into the machine.
5. Select the **"Sorbet"** mode and process.
6. If the texture is too firm or crumbly, add 1-2 tablespoons of acai juice and press Re-Spin for extra smoothness.
7. Serve immediately or store in the freezer with a lid for later.

Nutritional Information (Per Serving)
Calories: 155
Fats: 0.5g
Protein: 25g

Lemon Coconut Protein Sorbet

Time Needed to Prepare: 5 minutes
CREAMi Time: 3-4 minutes (plus Re-Spin if needed)
Number of Servings: 2

Ingredients List

- 1 cup of (150g) frozen pineapple chunks
- 1/2 cup of (120ml) unsweetened coconut water
- 1 scoop (30g) unflavored or vanilla whey protein isolate
- 1 tablespoon of allulose or monk fruit sweetener
- 1 teaspoon fresh lemon zest
- 1/2 teaspoon fresh lemon juice
- 1 tablespoon of unsweetened shredded coconut (for topping)

Instructions

1. In a blender, combine frozen pineapple, coconut water, protein powder, sweetener, lemon zest, and lemon juice. Blend until smooth.
2. Pour the mixture into a Ninja CREAMi pint and secure the lid.
3. Freeze for 24 hours until solid.
4. Once frozen, place the pint into the Ninja CREAMi and lock it into the machine.
5. Select the **"Sorbet"** mode and process.
6. If the texture is too firm or crumbly, add 1-2 tablespoons of coconut water and press Re-Spin for extra smoothness.
7. Serve immediately, topped with shredded coconut, or store in the freezer with a lid for later.

Nutritional Information (Per Serving)
Calories: 160
Fats: 1.5g
Protein: 25g

Passionfruit Orange Muscle Sorbet

Time Needed to Prepare: 5 minutes
CREAMi Time: 3-4 minutes (plus Re-Spin if needed)
Number of Servings: 2

Ingredients List

- 1 cup of (150g) frozen mango chunks
- 1/2 cup of (120ml) unsweetened orange juice
- 1 scoop (30g) unflavored or vanilla whey protein isolate
- 1 tablespoon of allulose or monk fruit sweetener
- 1 tablespoon of passionfruit pulp (fresh or frozen)
- 1/2 teaspoon fresh lime juice

Instructions

1. In a blender, combine frozen mango, orange juice, protein powder, sweetener, passionfruit pulp, and lime juice. Blend until smooth.
2. Pour the mixture into a Ninja CREAMi pint and secure the lid.
3. Freeze for 24 hours until solid.
4. Once frozen, place the pint into the Ninja CREAMi and lock it into the machine.
5. Select the **"Sorbet"** mode and process.
6. If the texture is too firm or crumbly, add 1-2 tablespoons of orange juice and press Re-Spin for extra smoothness.
7. Serve immediately or store in the freezer with a lid for later.

Nutritional Information (Per Serving)
Calories: 165
Fats: 0.5g
Protein: 25g

Blackberry Lime Whey Sorbet

Time Needed to Prepare: 5 minutes
CREAMi Time: 3-4 minutes (plus Re-Spin if needed)
Number of Servings: 2

Ingredients List

- 1 cup of (150g) frozen blackberries
- 1/2 cup of (120ml) unsweetened coconut water
- 1 scoop (30g) unflavored or vanilla whey protein isolate
- 1 tablespoon of allulose or monk fruit sweetener
- 1/2 teaspoon fresh lime zest
- 1/2 teaspoon fresh lime juice

Instructions

1. In a blender, combine frozen blackberries, coconut water, protein powder, sweetener, lime zest, and lime juice. Blend until smooth.
2. Pour the mixture into a Ninja CREAMi pint and secure the lid.
3. Freeze for 24 hours until solid.
4. Once frozen, place the pint into the Ninja CREAMi and lock it into the machine.
5. Select the **"Sorbet"** mode and process.
6. If the texture is too firm or crumbly, add 1-2 tablespoons of coconut water and press Re-Spin for extra smoothness.
7. Serve immediately or store in the freezer with a lid for later.

Nutritional Information (Per Serving)
Calories: 155
Fats: 0.5g
Protein: 25g

Tart Cherry Vanilla Recovery Sorbet

Time Needed to Prepare: 5 minutes
CREAMi Time: 3-4 minutes (plus Re-Spin if needed)
Number of Servings: 2

Ingredients List

- 1 cup of (150g) frozen tart cherries
- 1/2 cup of (120ml) unsweetened coconut water
- 1 scoop (30g) vanilla whey protein isolate
- 1 tablespoon of allulose or monk fruit sweetener
- 1/2 teaspoon vanilla extract
- 1/2 teaspoon fresh lemon juice

Instructions

1. In a blender, combine frozen tart cherries, coconut water, protein powder, sweetener, vanilla extract, and lemon juice. Blend until smooth.
2. Pour the mixture into a Ninja CREAMi pint and secure the lid.
3. Freeze for 24 hours until solid.
4. Once frozen, place the pint into the Ninja CREAMi and lock it into the machine.
5. Select the **"Sorbet"** mode and process.
6. If the texture is too firm or crumbly, add 1-2 tablespoons of coconut water and press Re-Spin for extra smoothness.
7. Serve immediately or store in the freezer with a lid for later.

Nutritional Information (Per Serving)
Calories: 160
Fats: 0.5g | **Protein:** 25g

Honeydew Green Tea Sorbet

Time Needed to Prepare: 5 minutes
CREAMi Time: 3-4 minutes (plus Re-Spin if needed)
Number of Servings: 2

Ingredients List

- 1 cup of (150g) frozen honeydew melon chunks
- 1/2 cup of (120ml) brewed and cooled green tea (unsweetened)
- 1 scoop (30g) unflavored or vanilla whey protein isolate
- 1 tablespoon of allulose or monk fruit sweetener
- 1/2 teaspoon fresh lime juice

Instructions

1. In a blender, combine frozen honeydew, green tea, protein powder, sweetener, and lime juice. Blend until smooth.
2. Pour the mixture into a Ninja CREAMi pint and secure the lid.
3. Freeze for 24 hours until solid.
4. Once frozen, place the pint into the Ninja CREAMi and lock it into the machine.
5. Select the **"Sorbet"** mode and process.
6. If the texture is too firm or crumbly, add 1-2 tablespoons of green tea and press Re-Spin for extra smoothness.
7. Serve immediately or store in the freezer with a lid for later.

Nutritional Information (Per Serving)
Calories: 150
Fats: 0.5g
Protein: 25g

Cucumber Melon Refresh Sorbet

Time Needed to Prepare: 5 minutes
CREAMi Time: 3-4 minutes (plus Re-Spin if needed)
Number of Servings: 2

Ingredients List

- 1 cup of (150g) frozen honeydew melon chunks
- 1/2 cup of (120ml) unsweetened coconut water
- 1/2 cup of (50g) peeled and chopped cucumber
- 1 scoop (30g) unflavored or vanilla whey protein isolate
- 1 tablespoon of allulose or monk fruit sweetener
- 1/2 teaspoon fresh lime juice

Instructions

1. In a blender, combine frozen honeydew, coconut water, cucumber, protein powder, sweetener, and lime juice. Blend until smooth.
2. Pour the mixture into a Ninja CREAMi pint and secure the lid.
3. Freeze for 24 hours until solid.
4. Once frozen, place the pint into the Ninja CREAMi and lock it into the machine.
5. Select the **"Sorbet"** mode and process.
6. If the texture is too firm or crumbly, add 1-2 tablespoons of coconut water and press Re-Spin for extra smoothness.
7. Serve immediately or store in the freezer with a lid for later.

Nutritional Information (Per Serving)
Calories: 145
Fats: 0.5g
Protein: 25g

CHAPTER 6: MILKSHAKES

Classic Vanilla Whey Power Shake

Time Needed to Prepare: 5 minutes
CREAMi Time: 2-3 minutes
Number of Servings: 2

Ingredients List

- 1 cup of (240ml) unsweetened almond milk or skim milk
- 1 scoop (30g) vanilla whey protein isolate
- 1 tablespoon of allulose or monk fruit sweetener
- 1/2 teaspoon vanilla extract
- 1/4 teaspoon xanthan gum (for thickness)
- 1/2 cup of (75g) ice cubes

Instructions

1. In a blender, combine almond milk, protein powder, sweetener, vanilla extract, xanthan gum, and ice cubes. Blend until completely smooth.
2. Pour the mixture into a Ninja CREAMi pint and secure the lid.
3. Place the pint into the Ninja CREAMi and lock it into the machine.
4. Select the **"Milkshake"** mode and process.
5. Serve immediately.

Nutritional Information (Per Serving)
Calories: 150
Fats: 2g
Protein: 27g

Double Chocolate Casein Shake

Time Needed to Prepare: 5 minutes
CREAMi Time: 2-3 minutes
Number of Servings: 2

Ingredients List

- 1 cup of (240ml) unsweetened almond milk or skim milk
- 1 scoop (30g) chocolate casein protein powder
- 1 tablespoon of unsweetened cocoa powder
- 1 tablespoon of allulose or monk fruit sweetener
- 1/2 teaspoon vanilla extract
- 1/4 teaspoon xanthan gum (for thickness)
- 1/2 cup of (75g) ice cubes

Instructions

1. In a blender, combine almond milk, casein protein powder, cocoa powder, sweetener, vanilla extract, xanthan gum, and ice cubes. Blend until completely smooth.
2. Pour the mixture into a Ninja CREAMi pint and secure the lid.
3. Place the pint into the Ninja CREAMi and lock it into the machine.
4. Select the **"Milkshake"** mode and process.
5. Serve immediately.

Nutritional Information (Per Serving)
Calories: 160
Fats: 3g
Protein: 29g

Peanut Butter Banana Recovery Shake

Time Needed to Prepare: 5 minutes
CREAMi Time: 2-3 minutes
Number of Servings: 2

Ingredients List

- 1 cup of (240ml) unsweetened almond milk or skim milk
- 1 scoop (30g) vanilla whey protein isolate
- 1 small ripe banana
- 1 tablespoon of natural peanut butter (no added sugar or oil)
- 1 tablespoon of allulose or monk fruit sweetener
- 1/2 teaspoon vanilla extract
- 1/4 teaspoon xanthan gum (for thickness)
- 1/2 cup of (75g) ice cubes

Instructions

1. In a blender, combine almond milk, protein powder, banana, peanut butter, sweetener, vanilla extract, xanthan gum, and ice cubes. Blend until completely smooth.
2. Pour the mixture into a Ninja CREAMi pint and secure the lid.
3. Place the pint into the Ninja CREAMi and lock it into the machine.
4. Select the **"Milkshake"** mode and process.
5. Serve immediately.

Nutritional Information (Per Serving)
Calories: 200
Fats: 5g
Protein: 28g

Cookies & Cream Whey Shake

Time Needed to Prepare: 5 minutes
CREAMi Time: 2-3 minutes
Number of Servings: 2

Ingredients List

- 1 cup of (240ml) unsweetened almond milk or skim milk
- 1 scoop (30g) cookies & cream whey protein isolate
- 1 tablespoon of allulose or monk fruit sweetener
- 1/2 teaspoon vanilla extract
- 1/4 teaspoon xanthan gum (for thickness)
- 1/2 cup of (75g) ice cubes
- 2 sugar-free chocolate sandwich cookies (crushed, for mix-in)

Instructions

1. In a blender, combine almond milk, protein powder, sweetener, vanilla extract, xanthan gum, and ice cubes. Blend until completely smooth.
2. Pour the mixture into a Ninja CREAMi pint and secure the lid.
3. Place the pint into the Ninja CREAMi and lock it into the machine.
4. Select the **"Milkshake"** mode and process.
5. Create a small well in the center of the shake and add the crushed cookies.
6. Place the pint back into the Ninja CREAMi and select the **"Mix-In"** function.
7. Serve immediately.

Nutritional Information (Per Serving)
Calories: 190
Fats: 4g
Protein: 28g

Strawberry Shortcake Protein Shake

Time Needed to Prepare: 5 minutes
CREAMi Time: 2-3 minutes
Number of Servings: 2

Ingredients List

- 1 cup of (240ml) unsweetened almond milk or skim milk
- 1 scoop (30g) vanilla whey protein isolate
- 1/2 cup of (75g) frozen strawberries
- 1 tablespoon of sugar-free vanilla pudding mix
- 1 tablespoon of allulose or monk fruit sweetener
- 1/2 teaspoon vanilla extract
- 1/4 teaspoon xanthan gum (for thickness)
- 1/2 cup of (75g) ice cubes
- 1 crushed sugar-free shortbread cookie (for mix-in)

Instructions

1. In a blender, combine almond milk, protein powder, frozen strawberries, pudding mix, sweetener, vanilla extract, xanthan gum, and ice cubes. Blend until completely smooth.
2. Pour the mixture into a Ninja CREAMi pint and secure the lid.
3. Place the pint into the Ninja CREAMi and lock it into the machine.
4. Select the **"Milkshake"** mode and process.
5. Create a small well in the center of the shake and add the crushed shortbread cookie.
6. Place the pint back into the Ninja CREAMi and select the **"Mix-In"** function.
7. Serve immediately.

Nutritional Information (Per Serving)
Calories: 195
Fats: 4g
Protein: 28g

Mocha Cold Brew Muscle Shake

Time Needed to Prepare: 5 minutes
CREAMi Time: 2-3 minutes
Number of Servings: 2

Ingredients List

- 1 cup of (240ml) unsweetened cold brew coffee
- 1 scoop (30g) chocolate whey protein isolate
- 1 tablespoon of unsweetened cocoa powder
- 1 tablespoon of allulose or monk fruit sweetener
- 1/2 teaspoon vanilla extract
- 1/4 teaspoon xanthan gum (for thickness)
- 1/2 cup of (75g) ice cubes

Instructions

1. In a blender, combine cold brew coffee, protein powder, cocoa powder, sweetener, vanilla extract, xanthan gum, and ice cubes. Blend until completely smooth.
2. Pour the mixture into a Ninja CREAMi pint and secure the lid.
3. Place the pint into the Ninja CREAMi and lock it into the machine.
4. Select the **"Milkshake"** mode and process.
5. Serve immediately.

Nutritional Information (Per Serving)
Calories: 160
Fats: 2g
Protein: 29g

Cinnamon Roll Oatmeal Shake

Time Needed to Prepare: 5 minutes
CREAMi Time: 2-3 minutes
Number of Servings: 2

Ingredients List

- 1 cup of (240ml) unsweetened almond milk or skim milk
- 1 scoop (30g) vanilla whey protein isolate
- 1/4 cup of (20g) rolled oats
- 1 tablespoon of sugar-free vanilla pudding mix
- 1 tablespoon of allulose or monk fruit sweetener
- 1/2 teaspoon ground cinnamon
- 1/2 teaspoon vanilla extract
- 1/4 teaspoon xanthan gum (for thickness)
- 1/2 cup of (75g) ice cubes

Instructions

1. In a blender, combine almond milk, protein powder, oats, pudding mix, sweetener, cinnamon, vanilla extract, xanthan gum, and ice cubes. Blend until completely smooth.
2. Pour the mixture into a Ninja CREAMi pint and secure the lid.
3. Place the pint into the Ninja CREAMi and lock it into the machine.
4. Select the **"Milkshake"** mode and process.
5. Serve immediately.

Nutritional Information (Per Serving)
Calories: 180
Fats: 3g
Protein: 28g

Dark Chocolate Cherry Power Shake

Time Needed to Prepare: 5 minutes
CREAMi Time: 2-3 minutes
Number of Servings: 2

Ingredients List

- 1 cup of (240ml) unsweetened almond milk or skim milk
- 1 scoop (30g) chocolate whey protein isolate
- 1/2 cup of (75g) frozen tart cherries
- 1 tablespoon of unsweetened cocoa powder
- 1 tablespoon of allulose or monk fruit sweetener
- 1/2 teaspoon vanilla extract
- 1/4 teaspoon xanthan gum (for thickness)
- 1/2 cup of (75g) ice cubes

Instructions

1. In a blender, combine almond milk, protein powder, frozen cherries, cocoa powder, sweetener, vanilla extract, xanthan gum, and ice cubes. Blend until completely smooth.
2. Pour the mixture into a Ninja CREAMi pint and secure the lid.
3. Place the pint into the Ninja CREAMi and lock it into the machine.
4. Select the **"Milkshake"** mode and process.
5. Serve immediately.

Nutritional Information (Per Serving)
Calories: 175
Fats: 3g
Protein: 28g

Chai Latte Collagen Shake

Time Needed to Prepare: 5 minutes
CREAMi Time: 2-3 minutes
Number of Servings: 2

Ingredients List

- 1 cup of (240ml) brewed and cooled chai tea (unsweetened)
- 1 scoop (30g) vanilla whey protein isolate
- 1 scoop (10g) unflavored collagen peptides
- 1 tablespoon of allulose or monk fruit sweetener
- 1/2 teaspoon ground cinnamon
- 1/4 teaspoon ground ginger
- 1/8 teaspoon ground cardamom
- 1/8 teaspoon ground cloves
- 1/2 teaspoon vanilla extract
- 1/4 teaspoon xanthan gum (for thickness)
- 1/2 cup of (75g) ice cubes

Instructions

1. In a blender, combine chai tea, protein powder, collagen peptides, sweetener, cinnamon, ginger, cardamom, cloves, vanilla extract, xanthan gum, and ice cubes. Blend until completely smooth.
2. Pour the mixture into a Ninja CREAMi pint and secure the lid.
3. Place the pint into the Ninja CREAMi and lock it into the machine.
4. Select the **"Milkshake"** mode and process.
5. Serve immediately.

Nutritional Information (Per Serving)
Calories: 165
Fats: 2g
Protein: 30g

Caramel Macchiato Whey Shake

Time Needed to Prepare: 5 minutes
CREAMi Time: 2-3 minutes
Number of Servings: 2

Ingredients List

- 1 cup of (240ml) unsweetened cold brew coffee
- 1 scoop (30g) vanilla whey protein isolate
- 1 tablespoon of sugar-free caramel syrup
- 1 tablespoon of allulose or monk fruit sweetener
- 1/2 teaspoon vanilla extract
- 1/4 teaspoon xanthan gum (for thickness)
- 1/2 cup of (75g) ice cubes

Instructions

1. In a blender, combine cold brew coffee, protein powder, caramel syrup, sweetener, vanilla extract, xanthan gum, and ice cubes. Blend until completely smooth.
2. Pour the mixture into a Ninja CREAMi pint and secure the lid.
3. Place the pint into the Ninja CREAMi and lock it into the machine.
4. Select the **"Milkshake"** mode and process.
5. Serve immediately.

Nutritional Information (Per Serving)
Calories: 160
Fats: 2g
Protein: 29g

Key Lime Pie Protein Shake

Time Needed to Prepare: 5 minutes
CREAMi Time: 2-3 minutes
Number of Servings: 2

Ingredients List

- 1 cup of (240ml) unsweetened almond milk or skim milk
- 1 scoop (30g) vanilla whey protein isolate
- 1 tablespoon of sugar-free vanilla pudding mix
- 1 tablespoon of allulose or monk fruit sweetener
- 1 teaspoon fresh lime zest
- 1 tablespoon of fresh lime juice
- 1/2 teaspoon vanilla extract
- 1/4 teaspoon xanthan gum (for thickness)
- 1/2 cup of (75g) ice cubes
- 1 crushed sugar-free graham cracker (for mix-in)

Instructions

1. In a blender, combine almond milk, protein powder, pudding mix, sweetener, lime zest, lime juice, vanilla extract, xanthan gum, and ice cubes. Blend until completely smooth.
2. Pour the mixture into a Ninja CREAMi pint and secure the lid.
3. Place the pint into the Ninja CREAMi and lock it into the machine.
4. Select the **"Milkshake"** mode and process.
5. Create a small well in the center of the shake and add the crushed graham cracker.
6. Place the pint back into the Ninja CREAMi and select the **"Mix-In"** function.
7. Serve immediately.

Nutritional Information (Per Serving)
Calories: 180
Fats: 3g
Protein: 28g

Pumpkin Spice Recovery Shake

Time Needed to Prepare: 5 minutes
CREAMi Time: 2-3 minutes
Number of Servings: 2

Ingredients List

- 1 cup of (240ml) unsweetened almond milk or skim milk
- 1 scoop (30g) vanilla whey protein isolate
- 1/4 cup of (60g) canned pumpkin puree (unsweetened)
- 1 tablespoon of sugar-free vanilla pudding mix
- 1 tablespoon of allulose or monk fruit sweetener
- 1/2 teaspoon pumpkin spice blend
- 1/2 teaspoon vanilla extract
- 1/4 teaspoon xanthan gum (for thickness)
- 1/2 cup of (75g) ice cubes

Instructions

1. In a blender, combine almond milk, protein powder, pumpkin puree, pudding mix, sweetener, pumpkin spice, vanilla extract, xanthan gum, and ice cubes. Blend until completely smooth.
2. Pour the mixture into a Ninja CREAMi pint and secure the lid.
3. Place the pint into the Ninja CREAMi and lock it into the machine.
4. Select the **"Milkshake"** mode and process.
5. Serve immediately.

Nutritional Information (Per Serving)
Calories: 175
Fats: 3g
Protein: 28g

MEASUREMENT CONVERSION TABLE

Measurement	Imperial (US)	Metric
Volume		
1 teaspoon	1 teaspoon	5 milliliters
1 tablespoon	1 tablespoon	15 milliliters
1 fluid ounce	1 fl oz	30 milliliters
1 cup	1 cup	240 milliliters
1 pint	1 pt	473 milliliters
1 quart	1 qt	0.95 liters
1 gallon	1 gal	3.8 liters
Weight		
1 ounce	1 oz	28 grams
1 pound	1 lb	454 grams
Temperature		
32°F	32°F	0°C
212°F	212°F	100°C
Other		
1 stick of butter	1 stick	113 grams

CONCLUSION

As you reach the final pages of this **Ninja CREAMi High-Protein Power Cookbook**, remember that this is not the end—it's just the beginning of your journey into delicious, nutritious, and protein-packed frozen creations. Whether you've been whipping up creamy **protein ice creams**, blending nutrient-dense **smoothie bowls**, or indulging in guilt-free **gelatos, sorbets, and shakes**, you've now unlocked the full potential of high-protein frozen treats.

Beyond Just Recipes—A Lifestyle

This cookbook isn't just about making healthier versions of your favorite desserts—it's about **fueling your body, supporting your fitness goals, and embracing a sustainable, protein-rich lifestyle**. With every scoop, every spoonful, and every sip, you are nourishing yourself with balanced macronutrients while indulging in flavors that make clean eating effortless and enjoyable.

Experiment, Innovate, and Enjoy

The recipes provided are just a foundation. **Feel free to experiment, swap ingredients, and tailor flavors** to suit your preferences. Whether you prefer plant-based proteins, collagen boosts, or a mix of whey and casein, the Ninja CREAMi empowers you to create desserts that align with your health and fitness goals.

Your Next Steps

Now that you've mastered the art of protein-packed frozen treats, share your creations, inspire others, and keep pushing the boundaries of what's possible in high-protein desserts. **Stay creative, stay healthy, and most importantly—enjoy every bite!**

Thank you for joining this **high-protein revolution**. Here's to a future filled with **delicious, nutritious frozen treats!**

RECIPES INDEX

Acai Superfood Protein Bowl 31

Apple Pie Cinnamon Protein Bowl 36

Berry Blast Greek Yogurt Protein Bowl 32

Birthday Cake Protein Ice Cream 17

Black Sesame Whey Gelato 42

Blackberry Lime Whey Sorbet 47

Blueberry Acai Superfood Sorbet 45

Blueberry Vanilla Whey Bowl 35

Caramel Macchiato Whey Shake 58

Chai Latte Collagen Shake 57

Chai Spice Protein Gelato 42

Chia & Flax Seed Crunch Ice Cream 24

Chocolate Almond Butter Energy Bowl 32

Chocolate Banana Recovery Ice Cream 16

Cinnamon Roll Oatmeal Shake 55

Cinnamon Roll Swirl Protein Ice Cream 15

Cinnamon Toasted Pecans Ice Cream 28

Classic Vanilla Whey Power Shake 49

Coconut Cashew High-Protein Gelato 39

Collagen-Boosted Granola Clusters Ice Cream 27

Cookies & Cream Muscle Ice Cream 14

Cookies & Cream Whey Shake 52

Crushed Freeze-Dried Berries Ice Cream 30

Crushed Protein Bar Chunks Ice Cream 20

Cucumber Melon Refresh Sorbet 48

Dark Chocolate Cherry Power Shake 56

Dark Chocolate Hazelnut Protein Gelato 37

Double Chocolate Casein Shake 50

Double Chocolate Fudge Protein Ice Cream 13

Espresso Macchiato Protein Gelato 38

Espresso-Cocoa Dusting Ice Cream 19

Green Machine Spinach Protein Bowl 33

High-Protein Brownie Bites Ice Cream 25

Honey Lavender Protein Gelato 40

Honeydew Green Tea Sorbet 48

Italian Vanilla Bean Whey Gelato 37

Key Lime Pie Protein Shake 59

Lemon Coconut Protein Sorbet 46

Lemon Ricotta Whey Gelato 41

Maple Pecan Crunch Protein Ice Cream 17

Maple Walnut High-Protein Gelato 41

Matcha Green Tea Protein Ice Cream 18

Mocha Cold Brew Muscle Shake 54

Mocha Espresso High-Protein Ice Cream 15

Mocha Oatmeal Protein Bowl 34

Oatmeal Cookie Protein Crumbles Ice Cream 26

Passionfruit Orange Muscle Sorbet 46

Peach Mango Collagen Sorbet 44

Peanut Butter Banana Muscle Bowl 33

Peanut Butter Banana Recovery Shake 51

Peanut Butter Cup Protein Ice Cream 14

Peanut Butter Drizzle (Low-Fat) Ice Cream 18

Pineapple Ginger Recovery Sorbet 43

Pistachio Almond Cream Gelato 38

Pumpkin Spice Recovery Shake 60

Raspberry Chocolate Swirl Protein Gelato 40

Raspberry Lemonade Whey Sorbet 43

Salted Caramel Whey Ice Cream 16

Strawberry Basil High-Protein Sorbet 45

Strawberry Cheesecake Protein Ice Cream 22

Strawberry Kiwi Power Bowl 35

Strawberry Shortcake Protein Shake 53

Sugar-Free Chocolate Chips & Cocoa Nibs Ice Cream 21

Sugar-Free Marshmallow Swirls Ice Cream 29

Tart Cherry Vanilla Recovery Sorbet 47

Tiramisu Collagen-Boosted Gelato 39

Toasted Coconut & Almonds Ice Cream 23

Tropical Mango Pineapple Protein Bowl 31

Vanilla Bean Protein Power Ice Cream 13

Vanilla Coconut Crunch Smoothie Bowl 34

Watermelon Mint Electrolyte Sorbet 44

Printed in Dunstable, United Kingdom

71843226R00045